SPIRITUAL MANUAL

A HANDBOOK FOR SPIRITUALIST CHURCHES AND THEIR MEMBERS

THE BOOK TREE
San Diego, California

First published 1948
by General Assembly of Spiritualists
New York

New material, revisions and cover
© 2006, 2012
The Book Tree
All rights reserved

ISBN 978-1-58509-265-9

Cover layout & design
Ben Riggs

Published by
The Book Tree
P.O. Box 16476
San Diego, CA 92176
www.thebooktree.com

We provide fascinating and educational products to help awaken the public to new ideas and
information that would not be available otherwise.
Call 1 (800) 700-8733 for our *FREE BOOK TREE CATALOG*.

We wish to acknowledge our grateful thanks to all those in the "Spirit World" and "On Earth Plane" who have so earnestly contributed to this manual.

This Manual is a handbook for our Ministers, Lecturers and Students for regular services and study. General Assembly of Spiritualists, State of New York

THE MANUAL COMMITTEE

Publisher's Disclaimer

CONTENTS

INTRODUCTION

What is a Spiritualist? A Spiritualist is a person who believes in the continuation of life after death and the communication with those on the other side for the advancement of civilization and personal growth. The highest teachings we receive from this other world are used to help us while we are here. A large number of Spiritualist churches exist around the world yet very little has been published by them or for them. That is the purpose of reprinting this book, first published in 1948 by a Spiritualist organization in New York, which we recently discovered still exist today. Due to the age of the material and the fact that organizations change over the years, this book should not necessarily be construed as being an accurate representation of what this organization is today. With that said, the information put forth in this book represents a fantastic general guide for any Spiritualist church, organization or individual, wherever they might be.

In the San Diego, California area there are a number od Spiritualist organizations that have made the value of Spiritualist thinking and practice clear to its members and to the publishers, the latter being inspired enough to reprint this title in an effort to spread these same ideas. The Fraternal Spiritual Church, its staff and members, especially Rev. Millie Landis, have all been a great inspiration, having carried on this work consistently for decades, in addition to The First Spiritualist Church of San Diego and an amazing Spiritualist community in Escondido known as Harmony Grove, in existence since 1896. It is not often that groups like this can be deservedly acknowledged beyond their inner circle, so we have done that here. We also know that similar groups exist like this all over the world, and regret that we do not know them well enough to mention by name.

3

This book covers virtually every area of Spiritualist thought and worship and provides a great overall view of what spiritualism is all about. Includes chapters on the Historical Background, Definitions of Mediumship, What is Spiritualism?, What do Spiritualists Believe?, Spiritual Healing, The Nature of the Spirit World, Prophecy and Mediumship, Recorded Spirit Manifestations in the Bible, Prophecy and Mediumship, and includes instructional texts for the ceremonial functions of marriage, funeral and christening services. This work is highly recommended as a complete guidebook for all Spiritualists worldwide.

Paul Tice
May, 2012

PREFACE

The General Assembly of Spiritualists is an ecclesiastical govern-
ing body, incorporated by special act of Legislature of the State of New
York, Laws of 1914, with jurisdiction in the several states of the
United States of America and the Dominion of Canada.

It is empowered to issue charters to churches and auxiliaries.

It is empowered to ordain ministers with the right to perform
the marriage ceremony and all other offices of the church.

It is empowered to issue certificates to mediums, missionaries and
clerical attendants.

It has the right to extend its operations to the several states of
the United States of America and the Dominion of Canada.

The status of its churches and ministers is the same as that of all
other religious denominations, having the highest authority that may
be vested by law in any religious body.

Its tenets are those contained in the Declaration of Principles as
accepted by the Spiritualists of the world.

It supports freedom of thought in religion, and adheres to the
American principle of separation of Church and State, opposing any
legislative effort of compulsory religious training in the public school
system.

It recognizes the demonstration of magnetic and spiritual healing
as one of the tenets of Spiritualism.

It recognizes the demonstration of the gift of prophecy, clairvoyance,
trance and other forms of mediumship.

It is governed by a Constitution duly adopted by a convention of
its member churches. Its policies between annual conventions of the
member churches, are formulated by a Board of Directors elected at
the annual convention.

The General Assembly believes in the advancement of the Spiritualist religion as an *idealistic, humanitarian, and inspiring movement,*
that gives aid to the sick, through spiritual healing, and aid to the
sound of body, by well founded hope and faith. The General Assembly
is firmly and permanently opposed to all fraudulent and dishonest
imitations of real mediumship, and to the sensational display thereof.
The ideal of the General Assembly is continually to raise the standards
of the Spiritualist movement, to encourage study classes, reading
courses, dissemination of Spiritualist literature, and research work, to
the end that others may learn of the reality of the Spirit World and its
meaning to mankind.

HISTORICAL BACKGROUND

The General Assembly of Spiritualists is a sovereign, self-governing ecclesiastical body, incorporated by special act of the Legislature of the State of New York, under Chapter 485, Laws of New York, 1914. Its earlier history as an organized religious body goes back to November 15, 1897, at which date it was incorporated as the New York State Association of Spiritualists. At the convention in Rochester, N. Y., on June 20, 1914, the delegates assembled, by unanimous vote, authorized changing the constitution, by-laws and name to General Assembly of Spiritualists, to conform with the Laws of New York, 1914, Chapter 485, Section 1, Chapter 53 of the Laws of 1909, entitled "An act in relation to religious corporations, constituting Chapter 51 of the consolidated laws," adding Article XIII, Spiritualist Churches, sections 262 to 273, inclusive. By this act Spiritualism for the first time was recognized by law as a religion with distinct powers conferred by the Legislature upon the General Assembly of Spiritualists. The first annual convention of the General Assembly of Spiritualists was held June 18, 19 and 20, 1915. The Board of directors consisted of Hiram R. Savage, East Aurora, N. Y., President; Frank Walker, Hamburg, N. Y., Secretary; Seymour J. Richardson, Lily Dale, N. Y.; Richard R. Schleusner, New York, N. Y.; Harriet M. Rathbun, New York, N. Y.; Matilda U. Reynolds, Troy, N. Y.; John F. Steckenreiter, New York, N. Y.; Charles J. Tucker, Rochester, N. Y.; Samuel Newman, Buffalo, N. Y. The original charter of the General Assembly of Spiritualists was signed by the above-named members of the board of directors, and recorded in Monroe County, N. Y., on October 19, 1915.

Hiram R. Savage was succeeded in the Presidency of the General Assembly of Spiritualists by John F. Steckenreiter of New York, N. Y., followed by William H. Burr of Rochester, N. Y.

On December 17, 1927, John Heiss of New York, N. Y., became President, having held that office to date.

At the convention in Buffalo, N. Y., June 19, 20 and 21, 1931, the delegates assembled, in order to preserve the lofty principles expressed by the pioneers of Spiritualism, the Spiritualist principle of universal brotherhood, and to protect our movement against encroachments of prejudice and sectarianism, voted to sever its affiliation with other groups. The Board of Directors was authorized to amend the certificate of incorporation and revise the Constitution and By-laws accordingly. The Board of Directors consisted of John Heiss, New York, N. Y., President; Matthew Stephenson, Albany, N. Y., Vice-President; Frederick W. Constantine, Buffalo, N. Y., Secretary; Everett F. Britz, New York, N. Y., Treasurer; Alexander J. McIvor-Tyndall, Lily Dale, N. Y.; Leila Williams, Syracuse, N. Y.; Howard Mason Pitman, Buffalo, N. Y.; Sarah Cushing, Lily Dale, N. Y.; Emily Doyle, Buffalo, N. Y. The necessary legal steps were duly consummated, papers signed by the above Directors, and filed, establishing the General Assembly of Spiritualists as a sovereign, self-governing ecclesiastical body, with executive power vested in the Board of Directors of the General Assembly of Spiritualists, with jurisdiction extended to the several states of the United States and the Dominion of Canada.

The Board of Directors of the General Assembly of Spiritualists at this printing are: Rev. John Heiss, President; Rev. Leighton Ayling, Vice-president; Rev. John Carlson, Treasurer; Everett F. Britz, Secretary; Rev. Sarah W. Cushing, Director; Rev. Leota Maxwell, Director; Rev. Lillian Bleser, Director; George S. Shirk, Director; Rev. Beulah H. Brown, Director.

PEOPLE VERSUS STRONG

In 1943 two Policewomen in plain clothes attended a religious service at one of the General Assembly's Churches in New York City. As *agents provocateurs,* the Policewomen sought and obtained prophecies of a personal nature which were delivered by the Pastor from the pulpit.

Thereupon the Policewomen caused the arrest of the Pastor on a charge of violating the New York statute against fortune telling. At the trial a City Magistrate found the Pastor guilty. (183 Misc. 291).

On appeal, the three Judges on a higher court unanimously affirmed the conviction. (183 Misc. 748).

Thereafter an appeal to the Court of Appeals, the highest New York State Court, resulted in a unanimous reversal of the conviction by the seven Judges on that high court. (294 N. Y. 930).

Since that decision no Pastor of a General Assembly Church has been arrested on a fortune telling charge to date.

DEFINITIONS AND EXPLANATIONS

1. Spiritualism is the Science, Philosophy and Religion of continuous life, based upon the demonstrated fact of communication, by means of mediumship, with those who live in the Spirit World.

2. A Spiritualist is one who believes, as part of his or her Religion, in the communication between this, and the Spirit World, by means of mediumship, and who endeavors to mould his or her character and conduct in accordance with the highest teaching derived from such communication.

3. A Medium is one whose organism is sensitive to vibrations from the Spirit World, and through whose instrumentality, Intelligences in that World are able to convey messages and produce phenomena of Spiritualism.

ORDER OF SERVICES

Hymn

Invocation

Reading of Declaration of Principles.

1. We believe in Infinite Intelligence.

2. We believe that the phenomena of nature, both physical and spiritual are the expression of Infinite Intelligence.

3. We affirm that a correct understanding of such expression and living in accordance therewith constitute true religion.

4. We affirm that the existence and personal identity of the individual continue after the change called "Death".

5. We affrm that communication with the so-called "Dead" is a fact, scientifically proven by the phenomena of Spiritualism.

6. We believe that the highest morality is contained in the "Golden Rule": "Whatsoever ye would that others should do unto you, do you also unto them."

7. We affirm the moral responsibility of the individual and that he makes his own happiness or unhappiness as he obeys or disobeys Nature's Physical and Spiritual laws.

8. We affirm that the doorway to reformation is never closed against any human soul, here or hereafter.

Address or Lecture

Hymn

Announcements and Offertory

Messages

Closing Hymn and Benediction

DEFINITIONS OF MEDIUMSHIP

1. Clairvoyance—The Spiritual or Psychic power to see beyond the ordinary physical sense of sight.

2. Clairaudience—The Spiritual or Psychic power to hear beyond the physical sense of hearing.

3. Full Trance—A condition in which a medium's consciousness is subjected to spirit influence.

4. Materialization—The power to bring into tangible or visible form spiritual beings and objects.

5. Independent Voice—The power to produce spirit voice without the aid of physical means.

6. Trumpet—The power to produce spirit voice with the aid of a trumpet for amplification.

7. Healing—The power of spirit through mediumship to heal mental, physical and spiritual ailments.

8. Automatic Writing—A condition in which a medium's writing arm is controlled by a spirit intelligence.

Spiritualism is a SCIENCE because it demonstrates the scientific phenomena which are the material means of communication between the two worlds. These phenomena, with their various manifestations, illustrate the means of manifestation, the *modus operandi,* through which is given the proof of personal survival.

Spiritualism is a PHILOSOPHY because it corroborates the testimony of the ages, speculating upon the existence of the immortal soul of man; it accepts the observed facts of the great sages of history, delivering to the present day the logical findings of what must be true concerning man's present and future estate.

Spiritualism is a RELIGION because it bases its teachings upon the belief in God the Creator, and upon the spiritual quality of man. It declares its hope to be in the "expression of Infinite Intelligence" as a standard of all known truth. It seeks to comply with all laws, Physical, Mental and Spiritual, which are the manifestations of God to the consciousness of man.

SPIRITUALISM TEACHES AND AFFIRMS:

It teaches our personal accountability and responsibility before God and man. ,

It affirms death to be a blessing and not the "curse of man", as theology has defined it.

It teaches that death is a natural law of the material; that through the operation of this law the soul is released from the laws of mortality.

It teaches the existence of man as a living soul in a mortal body.

It affirms the spiritual existence of man.

It teaches in a most practical way the Scriptural injunction "Whatsoever a man soweth that shall he also reap."

It teaches that spirit communication is proved by the means of mediumship—clairvoyance, clairaudience, clairsentience—the psychic faculties through which we perceive spirit personality.

It teaches that spiritual man is the offspring of God: created in His likeness and image.

It teaches the continued unfoldment of the psychic and spiritual faculties of man.

It affirms Spiritualism to be a religious philosophy which is the continuation of God's revealed laws. It declares personal immortality and unlimited progression both here and hereafter.

It brings within a practical experience the use and development of Spiritual Gifts (1st Corinthians, 12th chapter) which are the express manifestations of God's spiritual laws demonstrated through man. These "gifts" becoming, through knowledge of Spiritualism's philosophy, recognized and brought into use, thus fulfilling their divine purpose.

WHAT IS SPIRITUALISM?

By REV. CONVERSE E. NICKERSON

Copyright 1940 by Converse E. Nickerson

Most of us have a nodding acquaintance with Spiritualism. We have heard of its dark seances, its table-tipping, its mysterious rappings, and sundry other eerie and awesome happenings. Some of us, too, have not been averse to secretly practicing, or holding to, many of the strange beliefs of its adherents. We longed to test by our own experience, the powers that psychic mediums claimed to possess.

Sometimes there has come in the still, quiet moments, the thought that the dark and secret veil of death is after all but a thin and gentle curtain which, with slight effort, we could lift and gaze upon a scene of rapture and delight, with those we love, participants in its glory. We have so much wished that this were true. Knowing that curiosity is the chief aid to enlightenment, we have even dared to seek, as Saul of old, the aid of a medium (1 Samuel 28) in the half-frightened endeavor to set our minds at rest on the subject. Then, because we were members of some good old orthodox creed, which breathes of hell, devil, and damnation, we chided ourselves for our backsliding, and continued on in the old way of groping and darkness.

The anathema of the church raised the fear in our hearts and the love and longing to know once more the companionship of the departed became stifled. The broken heart and sorrow-ridden spirit within us found no relief from loneliness.

Are those we call dead not really dead? Is this life here on earth the beginning of the true existence that shall last throughout eternity? Philosophy has ever been man's method of questioning all things? The very bed-rock of all religions must be laid in such philosophic questioning. Jesus invited us to ask and he promises that we should receive [1 John 3:22]. What more earnest request have we than that of knowing about our future state?

Spiritualism is the only religion that directly affirms that the dead are alive. More properly let me state it, that the personalities of those who have passed through the change called death, do still live and manifest. Now then, since we are confessedly interested in the answering of this great world question, Spiritualism, because of its claims in the matter, must necessarily interest us. Some of us are, it is true, a bit leary of ghosts and dark cabinets and of walking tables and spooky hands in the dark, but we feel that when it comes to the matter, of the orthodox resurrectional morn, when "they that are asleep (in their graves) shall hear his voice and arise," there will be many ghosts, and we imagine we will seem more natural and not so much afraid. But we'll wait till then before drawing too near to the world of shadows.

Let us see if these Spiritualists have any logical foundation for their beliefs. I am sure that we may have free access to their Declaration of Eight Principles which they have adopted as the charter of Spiritualistic philosophy; we shall see what they contain in the way of common reasoning and how much in them accords with our own beliefs and ideals of religion:

First Principle: *We believe in Infinite Intelligence.*

The avowed assertion of every soul, except the heathen and the infidel, is that there is a supreme Creator and that He knoweth all things. Infinite Intelligence is a master name for Him. Such a title is both honorable and reverent. Who of a Christian religion does not believe in an Infinite Intelligence? The Scriptures proclaim that "He knoweth all things: He knoweth the hearts of men and all their secret thoughts. The times and the seasons are in His hand." He is called "Alpha and Omega," the beginning and the ending of all created things,—Infinite Intelligence! Yes, we believe this too.

Every religion must have a comprehensive framework; there must be, for its argument before the minds of the world, a thesis that will set forth some complete proclamation about the philosophy of life. Spiritualism cannot better begin such a thesis than with the proclamation that God is Infinite Intelligence.

In theology there is a tangled skein of supposition and mystery surrounding the doctrine of God; some say there is one God, some say He is three in one. Thus Father, Son, and Holy Ghost form a declaration that is atmospherically hazy. Jesus is often confused with the personal identity of God the Father. The master of Nazareth severely enjoined his followers to pray, not to him, but to his heavenly father. The one who came to him and called him "good master," he rebuked by saying "Why callest thou me good? there is none good but one, that is, God." *(Matthew 19: 17)* Jesus prayed in the garden of agony "My Father . . . thy will be done." *(Mat. 26: 42).*

Still Christians cannot see Jesus as the great spiritual teacher and example of righteousness apart from God the creator of the universe. The doctrine of the trinity has ever been a stumbling block and a confusion since man first began to associate personal redemption with a belief in the devil and a hell of fire and brimstone.

Scientifically we approach truth, and it must follow therefore that our final comprehension of God shall utter in splendid amazement that profound term of adoration and authority, *Infinite Intelligence.*

Second Principle: *We believe that the Phenomena of Nature, both Physical and Spiritual, are the Expression of Infinite Intelligence.*

The definition of "phenomena" as given in any standard dictionary is "appearances of things, especially unusual appearances"; or to be more explicit, "an unusual manifestation." Now it is rational to infer, from ordinary reasoning and orthodox sentiment, that God made everything in the earth, the sea, and the air; and since we have agreed that He is Infinite Intelligence, it is most certain that this old universe is completely under His absolute control.

The only other being supposed to have any hand in the doings of God and mortals is St. Lucifer *(Isa. 14: 12);* but years and erudition are gradually resolving him to a mythical Santa Claus which the former Christian Church held over poor sinners to force them into repentance. If by any slip of God's good judgment this hell-master got into the list of God's sacred creations, we must consider him a being under God's surveillance and an inferior personage.

God's high estimation of man which places man upon the pinnacle of the list of created things,—God's masterpiece,—is the sternest proof that there is no higher favored creature. How is it within our religious justice to assume that God has placed aught in the way of man's ultimate perfection? Dare we blaspheme Him thus in the face of all His goodness?

"All things were made by Him; and without Him was not made anything that was made." *(John 1.3.)*

No portion of created things can be outside of scientific law. All laws are of God, therefore every such expression of lighted intelligence must have its source in the Living God that made the heavens and the earth, and all that is in them. It is written that "in Him we live and move and have our being"; *(Acts 17: 28)* the being quality of all visible things,—and invisible things,—is of God; they are the expressions of Infinite Intelligence!

If then a new experience comes to mankind that reveals the presence of the souls of the departed, shall we not consider such an experience to be governed by scientific law? There are no laws in the universe that are outside of God's authority.

Spiritual phenomena, or psychic manifestation, if proved to exist, must be under the laws of God.

God has ever revealed Himself to man's intelligence through experience; and by experience has man tested all things that come within the scope of his knowledge. The mysteries of earth, sea, and air, are relentlessly becoming clear as man has forced by his reason the secrets which they held. This is exactly "God's word" and surely is as important for study as any set of Jewish manuscripts that ever existed.

Third Principle: *We Affirm That a Correct Understanding of Such Expression, and Living in Accordance Therewith, Constitute True Religion.*

Since all the expressions of the manifestation of created things,—including all laws, whether spiritual or physical,—are the expressions of Infinite Intelligence, then it is altogether proper and fitting that man correctly understand such creations and such laws.

If we are counseled to understand God and to seek His knowledge, it is best that we get true enlightenment; no knowledge will suffice unless it is complete. All phenomena, natural and spiritual, are of God, as has been said, but if we recognize only the natural phenomena and disregard the others, we are one-sided and our vision of religion is exceedingly narrow.

"Knowledge is power, and a wise man seeketh wisdom." From the earliest written record man has sought to know the truth about himself and his surroundings. Job said, "I would know for myself and not another." Jesus said "Ask, and it shall be given you; seek, and ye shall find; knock, and it shall be opened unto you. *(Mat. 7: 7).*

"God is a Spirit; and they that worship him must worship him in Spirit and in truth" *(John 4: 24)* is the Scriptural injunction. To worship Him in truth demands a correct understanding of psychic law and the recognition of His workings within the realm of the forces of spirit.

Jesus told the people that "Thou shalt love the Lord thy God with all thy heart, and with all thy soul, and with all thy mind. This is the first and great Commandment." *(Mat. 22: 37-8.)*

First we love God as a father, for we know that His wisdom and mercy and His love for us, make us secure. We know that nothing can pluck us out of His hand. Then we love Him with our inmost consciousness, for we are a part of Him and thus naturally and instinctively do we turn toward Him.

Only with our minds can we grasp intellectually. To know God intellectually is surely to praise and magnify Him. To become aware of the greatness of God through science and psychic manifestation is certainly to be filled with wonder and amazement at the great power and glory of God. With such an understanding of God the fear of death has vanished and the knowledge of life has just begun.

True religion is to know God.

Fourth Principle: *We affirm That the Existence and Personal Identity of the Individual Continue After the Change Called Death.*

This is rather a startling statement, to say the least. Though we have always been taught in a vague way that God takes safe care of those who pass from mortal sight, yet we seldom or ever think of them in any other light than that of shadowy beings; our weak vision cannot picture them as anything like the personalities which we know here on earth.

The greatest force of personal spirit is evidenced in personality. Its charm shines through the physical, transforming it into a being of light and dignity. Eyes are made brilliant, ears are made receptive, voice becomes vibrant, all by the presence of a spirit personality in the mortal body. When it leaves nothing of interest is left. It is a living thing, a magic thing,—a thing that is most wonderful and enthralling. It is the offspring of God; it is the image of God; it is immortal and ever enduring; it is spirit.

The texture of the physical, its movements, its shape and all things belonging to it, are in some mysterious way the result and outcome of the spirit that lives within. It is created hourly by the invisible and, I might say, the unconscious powers of spirit.

Two important truths present themselves: spirit personality is a fact to us in this life expression, and spirit personality is greater and vastly more important than is the physical body.

When we talk about the communication of the spirit, we simply declare that the personality has made itself known. This is true not only of spirits out of the physical body, but of those still in the physical body.

Is it possible to see the so-called dead in dreams?

Your experiences and mine, in that way, prove to us beyond personal doubt that we have seen what we shall ever believe to have been likenesses of persons we once knew in the flesh. We bring back from such experiences correct details of the appearances of those images seen; we seem to have talked and acted with them in as real a manner as when we knew them in this life.

This proves to us that we have faculties other than the commonly accepted five senses, and that these faculties are as capable of recording facts as are those of waking consciousness. It seems reasonable that while the body sleeps we can attain control of these other senses, namely the "psychic senses"; clairvoyance (psychic sight) and clairaudience (psychic hearing), etc., which point directly to the faculties of spirit being.

These sleep-visions are closely related to the trance condition. It is possible to be in a trance state even while apparently awake. An accepted fact in Bible chronicles of trance is that of Peter who "went up to the house top to pray"; and "he fell into a trance." *(Acts 10: 9-16)*. The account of his vision which contained the spirit communication from a personality in the spirit world is fully related in those verses of Acts.

The fact that Peter had refused to preach to the Gentiles, just previous to this, had much to do with the nature of his vision; also the fact that he was hungry is of equal importance. This shows plainly the close relationship of the psychic trance conditions.

Every age and every people carry the recorded experiences of the communications of the spirit world with the world of mortals. Upon the hope that spirit personality is immortal hangs all the Christian religion and all the philosophy of religion that man cherishes.

To take away from man his hope of a future life is to blast and destroy the light of the ages. True faith in God is inseparable from the hope of immortality.

Fifth Principle: *We Affirm That Communication with the So-called Dead is a Fact Scientifically Proven by the Phenomena of Spiritualism.*

First let me state bluntly that the Spiritualists are the only people who have declared that they have communicated with the spirits of the so-called dead. Other spiritually minded denominations fully express their hope in further association with those loved on earth, but none have dared to attest communication.

There comes the weak objection that God does not intend us today to communicate with those whom He has called Beyond. The explanation is given that the saints of old who trod this earth seeing and doing wonderful things, were especially ordained by God to have special talks with the departed and with His ministering angels. This is not true. This is a hasty and thoughtless objection. The Bible has many commands against wizardry and the communication with evil spirits, but I have failed to find, after a careful search, any injunction against communing with wise spirit advisers, whenever such communication can be established. I know that many times some of the supposedly most sacred of the saints made most grievous mistakes by seeking and heeding the counsel of evil and crafty spirit visitors. This is often done today in our generation, for we are not always careful to "try the spirits." In I John 4:1 we read: "Beloved, believe not every spirit, but try the spirits whether they are of God; because many false prophets are gone out into the world." Had the old leaders of Israel known this advice of John's, a lot of their mistakes would not have been made.

Now, this Spiritualist doctrine is embedded in phenomena and its phenomena are positively proven by comparison with the psychic accounts given in the Old and New Testaments. That is one point in its favor.

The Bible records innumerable psychic phenomena, including materializations and communications between the living and the departed. Perhaps the most outstanding of such incidents is the one which occurred during the transfiguration of Jesus on the mountain, recorded in Mat. 17, Mark 9 and Luke 9.

On that occasion Jesus selected his three most mediumistic disciples, Peter, James and John, and he led them up into the solitude of the mountain to pray.

"And he was transfigured before them, and his face did shine as the sun, and his raiment was as white as the light." Evidently his body was covered with luminous ectoplasm, as happens in modern times.

"And, behold, there appeared unto them" the deceased "Moses and Elias talking with him."

"Then answered Peter, and said unto Jesus, Lord, it is good for us to be here; if Thou wilt, let us make here three tabernacles* (cabinets) ; one for Thee, and one for Moses and one for Elias."

"Behold, a bright (ectoplasmic) cloud overshadowed them; and behold a (direct) voice out of the cloud, which said, 'This is my beloved son, in whom I am well pleased.' "

"And when the disciples heard it, they fell on their face and were sore afraid. And Jesus came and touched them and said, Arise, and be not afraid. And when they had lifted up their eyes, they saw no man, save Jesus only."

"And as they came down from the mountain, Jesus charged them, saying, Tell the vision to no man, until the Son of man be risen again from the dead."

On the above mentioned occasion Jesus, Peter, James and John indubitably communicated with the deceased Moses and Elias, if the Bible is to be believed.

Moreover, time and again in modern times, the materialized forms of the departed have appeared at seances and have spoken audibly with those still in the flesh.

The seance on the Mount of Transfiguration and the modern instances of the same kind are mutually confirmatory.

Jesus performed no miracle outside of psychic law.

Psychic communication with the departed spirit must depend upon psychic law. We cannot use those former laws of the flesh to reach a being that is no longer bound to earth and its vibrations. The spirit within us, through thought and its kindred laws, which are psychic, can and does vibrate to waves of contact with such spirit planes as they inhabit.

Mediumship, simply a developed condition of super sensitivity, is the border-land between earthconsciousness and the spirit world. Thought transference is in daily use by normal mortals. We use many forms of its communication. Sight, hearing, and feeling, are always with us and through such avenues, the senses, we communicate with voice, vision, and gesture. All this is done through the air by the vibra-

---

*Charles Cutler Torrey, Professor of Semetic Languages at Yale University, translates tabernacles in his *The Four Gospels*, (1933) as "booths or shelters."

James Moffatt, D.D., Professor of Greek at Oxford, and later of Union Theological Seminary in New York City, translates it as "tents" in his *The New Testament. A New Translation*. 1922.

These translations appear to be good descriptions of the cabinets used by modern mediums during the production of ectoplasmic phenomena, including full form materalizations.

tory laws that surround us. Carried to a higher and more sensitive plane, shall we not be able, by the employment of finer and clearer receptive instruments, to reach to those who no longer use the vibrations of earth and the things of earth? Such receptive instruments we have in psychic mediumship. God has placed these powers at our disposal.

The powers of the psychic have long been under the careful scrutiny of science. The judgment and verdict of Oliver Lodge, or William Stead, or any other prominent man in their class, is not to be scoffed at or turned indifferently aside.

Edison and Marconi have so completely transcended all knowledge of Bible science, and have replaced Solomon's candles and David's messengers with such marvelous inventions, that civilization no longer fears to go forth in the seeking of knowledge which lies just a little beyond.

Every grandmother, nearly, can tell tales of mysterious happenings and spirit-rappings. Spiritualism makes no stranger of these things.

Sixth Principle: *We Believe That the Highest Morality is Contained in the Golden Rule: Whatsoever Ye Would That Others Should Do Unto You, Do Ye Also Unto Them.*

Jesus plainly taught, "As ye sow, so shall ye also reap."

Its logic is plain and it is but another way of saying that the Golden Rule is compellingly to be observed.

God's laws are just: spiritual equity demands only the quality of justice. What we deserve, that shall we receive if the spiritual scales are to be rightly balanced. If we set in motion any contrary vibration through unkindness, injustice, greed, envy, strife, or any other false vibration, it is the law of spirit, that we hurt ourselves and take away from our own wholeness and completeness. Our true quality is weakened by the wrong and thus we reap a harvest of effect that has come under false vibration.

Jesus taught the laws of righteousness. They are not of doctrinal Christianity as bound up in a church creed; they are universal spiritual laws that must affect all nations and creeds. Righteousness is the opposite to the evil, the false, the things lacking in justice and truth. The Golden Rule but emphasizes the spiritual command that we use the principles of justice in our quest for love and consideration as we journey through life.

Upon that principle rests the basis of all Christian and civil laws;

courtliness and civility are grounded knee-deep in its moral cement. The man who is totally indifferent to the kind of treatment he receives from his fellow men, is not caring much how he treats those about him; but if he learns that cause and effect are a part of the spiritual laws of justice then he will be most careful what kind of seed he is sowing. Like attracts like. In proportion to the observance of this rule has come the social regard and love which the world enjoys today. Morally this Sixth Principle of the Spiritualist philosophy holds sound "all ways from Sundays."

Seventh Principle: *We Affirm the Moral Responsibility of the Individual, and That He Makes His Own Happiness or Unhappiness As He Obeys or Disobeys Nature's Psychic Laws.*

Man is a free moral agent; his acts are, with the exception of the major events of his destiny, within his regulation. Now, no prize is worth having if it is unearned; a heaven of passive content is a hell to an active and progression-thirsting spirit. Worthiness is tested by the persistence and sincerity expended in pursuit of the prize. God's plan is man's perfection, and man's perfection is attained only by progression. Progression ceases when we stop striving, so to overcome moral and spiritual shortcoming we must strive, aim high, and work.

Love is the remedy and the example. Selfishness is opposed to love. Most of us have learned that we enjoy little without sharing it with others; that is how love's spiritual law works; it spends and gives unceasingly. How dull is a meal that we must eat alone. How cheery and beneficial does it become when we share it with another.

When Jesus taught us to "love one another" he gave us therewith a complete passport into heaven. All the responsibility for our partaking, or our neglecting to partake, of divine bliss rests upon our unfolding of that love; we are capable of the highest attainment of spiritual things, for we are the off-spring of God. You must change the living of a man before he can have a change of heart. Not only "all the way to heaven is heaven," but all the way must be made heaven! Decidedly must man make his own heaven; were God to deal otherwise with His offspring it would not be justice either to man or to God.

Jesus lived and continued to point the way to perfection until the world became so ashamed of its sin and hypocrisy that it turned upon its reprover and nailed Him to the cross of Calvary.

The Bible affirms that man is judged according to the deeds done in the body. This doctrine allows of no sacrifice for the absolution of sin. Sin is undeveloped good; sin is a state of ignorance of Divine Law. The spiritually awakened man seeks righteousness; he shuns even the appearance of evil; he knows that to be good he must do good. Always as the human race has spiritually awakened it has become finer grained and clearer visioned.

God has not damned any one; His greatest wish and delight is that man acknowledge the divine spiritual nature from which he sprang, and so obey its laws and reap its benefits.

Eighth Principle: *We Affirm That the Doorway to Reformation is Never Closed Against Any Human Soul, Here or Hereafter.* The strength of this statement is in its justice. Infinite Love and

Mercy cannot admit of any other conclusion to man's estate than complete reformation.

Every created soul is precious in the sight of Almighty God. The all-wise Father has no eternal black sheep in His fold. Sin is largely committed through ignorance. God knows this and He also knows that seventy or a hundred years is a short time in which to expect man to reach perfection.

The subject of forgiveness is a big consideration in the system of religious philosophy. In the striving after perfection man encounters sin, or imperfection. In comparing man with God, there we find the difference between the experiment with an awakening spiritual nature which seeks to know God, and the Divine Mind which has created man with spiritual desires.

God will forgive man as often as he shall seek forgiveness, though it be throughout eternity.

The Psalmist has said, "His love and mercy endureth forever."

The reasoning mind will see that the moment repentance takes place, forgiveness is. What prayer for the remission of sin can be as sacred in the sight of God as that sincere moment of repentance; that moment when the soul realizes its need for forgiveness and spiritual light.

The parables of Jesus are full of examples of a father's forgiveness. "If ye then, being evil, know how to give good gifts unto your children, how much more shall your Father which is in heaven give good things to them that ask him?" *(Mat. 7: 11)*

The Prodigal Son is an apt illustration of the great forgiving love of God. Can you imagine a true father ever casting aside his offspring? Some will say that the Prodigal Son first sought his father's forgiveness. So will every one of us do as soon as we realize that we have sinned and come short of the glory of God. Some time, here or hereafter, every one shall work out his own salvation, yea, though he do it with fear and trembling, for the doorway of reformation is never closed against any human soul, here or hereafter.

"Add to your Faith . . . Knowledge." *(2 Peter 1:5)* "And ye shall know the Truth, and the Truth shall make you Free." *(John 8:32).*

WHAT DO SPIRITUALISTS BELIEVE?

By Paul R. Lomaxe

Copyright 1943 by General Assembly of Spiritualists

The greatest difference between the beliefs of Spiritualists and other faiths, is their belief in the fact of communication between the living and the departed. They believe, with John, when he said, "Beloved, believe not every spirit, but try the spirits whether they are of God." I John 4:1.

Two well known instances of communication with the dead are:

"Jesus taketh with him Peter, James and John and leadeth them up into a high mountain apart by themselves . . . And there appeared unto them Elias, with Moses; and they were talking with Jesus." Mark 9:2-4, Mat. 17:3, Luke 9:30.

The wicked Saul, who tried to murder David with a javelin, later consulted "a woman that hath a familiar spirit." At Saul's request, she brought up Samuel who said, "Why hast thou disquieted me, to bring me up?" Samuel added a prophecy that Saul and his sons would die the next day. And the prophecy was fulfilled. I Samuel 18:10-11, 28:3-19, 31:1-5.

That great educator and publicist, the late Charles W. Eliot, president of Harvard University for forty years, said on July 22, 1909, at a lecture at the Harvard Summer School of Theology, "It" — the Religion of the Future — "will have its communions, with the Great Spirit, *with the spirits of the departed,* and with living fellowmen of like minds."

The Rev. Spence Jones, Dean of Gloucester, studied the very numerous early Christian inscriptions on the walls of the Catacombs. After having read hundreds of them, the Dean wrote, "The early Christians speak of the dead as though they were still living. They talk to their dead."

Saint Augustine, (354-430 A.D.), one of the early Christian Bishops and church fathers, says in his *De cura pro Mortuis,* "The spirits of the dead can be sent to the living and can unveil to them the future which they themselves have learned from other spirits or from angels" (i.e., spiritual guides) "or by divine revelation."

Tertullian is the earliest and, after Augustine, the greatest of the ancient church writers of the West. When he had his great controversy with the Marcionite sect, in the second century, he made the spiritual gifts (I Corin. 12) the test of truth between the two parties.

He claimed that these were forthcoming in greater profusion upon his own side, and included among them trance utterance, prophecy, and revelation of secret things. In his *De Anima* Tertullian says, "We have to-day among us a sister who has received gifts on the nature of revelations which she undergoes in spirit in the church amid the rites of the Lord's Day, falling into ecstacy (trance). She converses with angels" — that is, high spirits — "sees and hears mysteries, and reads the hearts of certain people and brings healings to those who ask. 'Among other things,' she said, 'a soul was shown to me in bodily form, and it seemed to be a spirit, but not empty nor a thing of vacuity. On the contrary, it seemed as if it might be touched, soft, lucid, of the colour of air, and of the human form in every detail'." The latter appears to be an example of the spiritual gift of "discerning of spirits" enumerated by St. Paul. I Corin. 12:10.

Adolph von Harnack, the well-known German theologian, wrote that in each early Christian Church there were three discreet women, one for healing and two for prophecy.

Spiritualists believe in *communion,* in the sense of communication with the departed, because they are able to communicate with the dead, just as the ancients testify that they communicated many centuries ago.

In fact, there is abundant evidence, both inside and outside of the Bible, to show that the beliefs of modern Spiritualism are identical with the beliefs of the early Christian Church. That subject, however, is too large to treat adequately within the limits of this paper.*

St. Paul wrote that man has a "natural body" and a "spiritual body," and that he is "raised a spiritual body." 1 Cor. 15:44. He also said that man is a *triune* being, in that he consists of (1) a spirit, (2) a soul (or spiritual body), and (3) a (physical) body. 1 Thes. 5:23. Moreover, it appears from the unknown author of the Epistle to the Hebrews that a distinction between soul (or spiritual body) and spirit is clearly recognized. Thus in Hebrews 4:12, we read, "For the word of God is quick, and powerful, and sharper than any two-edged sword, piercing even to *the dividing asunder of soul and spirit.*" Spiritualists believe that man is a *triune* being, not merely because it was so written in the New Testament many centuries ago,

---

* This subject may be pursued further by a reading of Dr. Abraham Wallace's little book, *Jesus of Nazareth;* Eugene Crowell's *The Identity of Primitive Christianity with Modern Spiritualism,* 1874, 2 vols.; and William Howitt's *The History of the Supernatural,* 1863, 2 vols.

but because they receive the same information here and now.

They believe that death consists merely of discarding one's physical body, like a worn out garment, and that the individual continues as a *dual* being, consisting of a spiritual body and a spirit.

Communications have been received from the so-called "dead," describing their sensations and experiences at the time of passing. As death approaches, all physical pain gradually ceases, and a great calm, peace and serenity overspreads the dying. Usually consciousness slowly fades away, and there is a period of the sleep of death, varying from a few minutes to days. Then consciousness gradually returns. In some instances, consciousness is not lost at all. Spiritualists, therefore, believe that Paul spoke truly, when he said, "We shall not all sleep, but we shall all be changed, in a moment, in the twinkling of an eye." 1 Cor. 15:51-2.

Shortly before death, the spiritual body retreats from the extremities, and moves slowly toward the head, at which point it leaves the physical body. But it is still connected to the old physical body by a magnetic cord which is invisible to our physical eyes. This cord soon pulsates and vibrates, and detaches itself from the physical body and becomes absorbed in the spiritual body. This is the moment of death,— the moment at which we are "changed in the twinkling of an eye," of which St. Paul speaks. The departed have so described the process of death, and clairvoyants on this side have witnessed it. What we call death is, on the other side, called birth.

John Pierpont, the spirit guide of Mrs. Mary E. Longley, the well known medium of former years, witnessed a death and reported it as follows:

"She is drifting out of the body; the silver cord is loosening its hold; the earth power is waning in power and the spirit body is forming for the change. A pearly vapor is gradually passing from the body; like a light mist, it collects around her head and rises upward. Now, the emanation increases in volume and in vibrant force and is issuing from the head. It is all condensing above the body, and gradually assuming the shape of a human form, till finally a complete resemblance to the woman on the bed is floating above. Now there is only a slight attachment by the silvery cord which has become very thread like and attenuated. Breathing to the watchers seems to have ceased, but the work is still going on, and does so until the cord is entirely loosened and, in its ethereal elements, is absorbed by the spirit body."

Hudson Tuttle, the medium, clairvoyantly witnessed, while in trance, (see Acts 10:10, 11:5, 22:17), a death and described it as follows:

"Slowly the spiritual form withdrew from the extremities and concentrated in the brain. As it did so, a halo arose from the crown of the head which gradually increased. Soon it became clear and distinct, and I observed that it had the exact resemblance of the form it had left. Higher and higher it arose, until the beautiful spirit stood before us and the dead body reclined below. A slight cord connected the two, which, gradually diminishing, became in a few minutes absorbed and the spirit had forever quitted its earthly temple."

To the vision of spirits, and to the clairvoyants who have seen it, this magnetic cord appears silvery. It is doubtless what is alluded to in the Biblical passage in Ecclesiastes, 12:6-7, as follows: "Or ever *the silver cord* be loosed . . . then shall the dust return to the earth as it was; and the spirit shall return unto God who gave it."

When consciousness returns to the newly-born spirit, he finds himself to be exactly the same person, knows that he is himself, has the same moral (or immoral) character, the same memory, knowledge, reason, prejudices, loves, hates, jealousies, and so on. His spiritual body is a replica of his discarded physical body, and, to his perception, it is just as substantial and real as his old physical body was.

Upon awaking from the sleep of death, some spirits, especially the unspiritual, the materialists and the atheists, who had not believed in a future life, are unable to comprehend that they have "died." They are bewildered and often think that they are dreaming. Instances are recorded of such spirits, upon seeing someone whom they knew to be dead, being frightened, thinking that they saw a ghost. Many are unable to understand their condition even when argued with; and some continue to wander in this unhappy and bewildered condition, sometimes for very long periods.

Several examples may be cited:

Dr. John W. Draper, the surgeon, who had not been over very long, said through the "direct voice," " . . . . What I want to know is, am I dreaming? I am sure I am dreaming. Tell me I am dreaming. The people around me are trying to tell me I have passed over, and I know it is not so. I must be dreaming, because I seem to be doing things, and I know I could not be doing things if I were dead."

About a month later he said, "This is Draper speaking, yes, Dr. Draper. Thanks for the help your (deceased) father-in-law has given me. You know I thought I was dreaming. I could not believe that I had died and was still alive. I never had any proof of continued existence, and I have operated on many. What is the use of surgeons operating on people and never discovering this? Now I am stronger than any x-ray I ever used. I can pass through stone walls. I can pass under water. Nothing can stop me."

The Reverend Doctor Floyd W. Tomkins was rector of the Church of Holy Trinity at Philadelphia. During his lifetime, some of his friends told him about conditions after death. But he found himself unable to believe it. After Dr. Tomkins' death, the deceased Dr. Clarke communicated, "At present he (Dr. Tomkins) thinks he is dreaming, but he will be all right. Perhaps he will speak to you tonight, he is here. Your mother has brought him here to show him that it is possible to speak to earth, and to prove to him that he is not dreaming." Later the same evening, exactly one week after his passing, Dr. Tomkins said in a faint voice, "Floyd Tomkins. Tell Sally her mother met me. Everything is as you told me it would be."

"All of them (spirits) agree," as Sir Arthur Conan Doyle points out, "that this state of bewilderment is harmful and retarding to the spirit, and that some knowledge of the actual truth upon this side is the only way to make sure of not being dazed upon the other. Finding conditions entirely different from anything for which either scientific or religious teaching has prepared them, it is no wonder that they look upon their new sensations as some strange dream, and the more rigidly orthodox have been their views, the more impossible do they find it to accept these new surroundings with all that they imply."

Dr. Carl A. Wickland reports, for example, the case of the Rev. J. O. Nelson, a Protestant minister, who had been killed *suddenly* by being hit by a train. He was in a dazed and bewildered condition for eight years before he came to a realization that he had died. Three years after his enlightenment he communicated, saying that he had progressed, and added, "I am happy, but I have a great deal to do."

Stewart Edward White's deceased wife, Betty, had been a medium in life, and both she and her husband had had an understanding of conditions on the other side. During the fighting in Poland at the beginning of the present World War II, she communicated to her husband, "We are all of us working so hard on people who are coming over *suddenly* now. Our friend the" — deceased — "Doctor is helping on that. He and I are working together. It is all confused here now; *so many coming suddenly, and they don't know what has happened to them.* You see, to people like you, and me when I left you" (died), "who know the facts of the very narrow no-man's land between what you call life" on earth "and what I now call life" in the spirit world — "well, we can" — at the time of our passing over — "aid those who come out to help us in going over, and meet them all clean and glorious and sure. Always those who go naturally are met and told what the change is, so that there is no disconcertion on their part. But those like you and me, we can help of our own volition and knowledge" when we pass over. "We are not only spared the surprise of finding ourselves suddenly in another sphere, but we ourselves can wipe out the tensions of our memories." This communication endorses the age-old plea of the Litany: "from battle . . . and *sudden* death, Good Lord, deliver us."

Some spirits are earthbound. They are held among earthly mortals, sometimes for incredibly long periods. They are not necessarily evil. "For where your treasure is, there will your heart be also." Mat. 6:21. An overwhelming motherly love, for instance, may keep a mother hovering around her surviving child. On the other hand, a dope fiend's terrible craving may cause him to frequent his earthly haunts in an effort to satisfy his urge for morphine.

There is no judge on the bench who pronounces sentence on, or awards favors to, each spirit as he arrives. In this life all of us build up our record by our conduct and our motives. We are selfish or unselfish, moral or immoral, in different degrees. We may be cruelly wicked or almost saintly. Whatever our spiritual status at death may be, *we* have made it.

After death, we gravitate automatically, so to speak, to the condition and companionship to which our moral character entitles, or condemns, us. In their earthly lives, "birds of a feather flock together," and it is the same on the other side.

Light, in the next life, is the measure of one's moral status. The wicked find themselves in darkness. The degree of darkness corresponds to their degree of wickedness.

Ancient scriptural writings show that, in Biblical days, the authors had an understanding of the importance of light and darkness in the next life. Several examples are here given:

In three instances, Jesus indicated that the punishment for misconduct is to be cast out "into outer darkness: there shall be weeping and gnashing of teeth." Mat. 22:13, 25:30, 8:12.

"Cast them down to hell, and deliver them into chains of darkness." 2 Peter 2:4.

"Are not my days few? Cease then, and let me alone, that I may take comfort a little, before I go whence I shall not return, even to the land of darkness and the shadow of death; a land of darkness, as darkness itself; and of the shadow of death, without any order, and where the light is as darkness." Job 10:20-22.

"He shall go to the generation of his fathers; they shall never see light." Psalms 49:19.

In one of the books of the Apocryphal New Testament, an ancient Christian document, it is written, "When we were placed with our fathers in the depths of hell, in the blackness of darkness." Gospel of Nicodemus 13:3.

"The wicked shall be silent in darkness." 1 Sam. 2:9.

Moreover, the Litany for the Dying beseeches the Lord "to give him joy and gladness in thy kingdom, with thy saints *in light.*"

A modern communication, on the subject of light, is:

"Light and darkness are states of the spirit, as you know. When those dwelling in the darkness cry for light, that means that they are become out of touch with their environment. So we send them what help is needed; and that is usually direction by which they find their way — not into regions of light, where they would be in torture, and utterly blinded, but — into a region less dark, and tinctured by just so much light as they can bear until they outgrow that state and cry in their longing for more.

"When a spirit leaves a dark region for one less dark, he experiences an immediate sense of relief and comfort by comparison with his former state. For now his environment is in harmony with his own inner state of development. But as he continues to develop in aspiration after good, he gradually becomes out of harmony with his surroundings, and then, in ratio to his progress, to his discomfort increases until it becomes not less than agony. Then in his helplessness, and approaching near to despair, having come to that pass where his own endeavors can go no further, he cries for help to those who are able to give it in God's name, and they enable him one stage onward nearer to the region where dimness, rather than darkness, reigns. And so he at last comes to the place where light is seen to be light; and his onward way is henceforth not through pain and anguish, but from joy to greater joy, and hence to glory and greater glory still.

"But oh, the long, long ages some do take until they come into that light, ages of anguish and bitterness; and know all the time that they may not come to their friends, who want them, until their own unfitness is done away; and that those great regions of darkness and lovelessness must be trod."

Good people, who have been unselfish and well intentioned, and have had love and sympathy for their fellowmen, arrive at death in a light which is at least equal to our light on earth. As they grow in unselfishness, in spirituality and in love, they progress onward to greater light. So, from the greatest depths of utter darkness, there is an eternal progression toward the light. Every spirit, however wicked, *eventually* gets to the light and beyond. This is the great *Law of Progression* of a loving God, who permits everyone to work out his own salvation, and not the law of a fiendish God who condemns some to *eternal* torture.

Upon awaking from the sleep of death, the spiritual bodies of the spirits in darkness are often crippled and in an unlovely condition. The bodies of those in the light are replicas of their discarded physical bodies. Deformities are corrected and lost limbs are restored. All elderly spirits, as they progress, grow younger in appearance until they reach a condition similar to that of the prime of life on earth; and deceased children grow up to a similar state. As they progress further, they become more beautiful and radiant.

No spirit progresses until it has the *desire*. Unless this knowledge of the possibility of progression had been obtained in earth life, there is naturally some time interval before an understanding of this truth is acquired in the next life. Many refuse to believe it when told. Others find conditions passably satisfactory to themselves, and are too lazy to make the effort. In some cases almost incredibly long periods elapse before progression is begun. As a communication, reported by Mrs. Drouet, states, "It is necessary that one should have desire, because in the spirit world, progression depends entirely upon the individual desire. Without desire for development, the spiritual man stagnates, and there are millions of souls here . . . who are floating about, because of that very lack of desire, to do, to be."

Spirits, who have acquired enough understanding and enlightment, pray when they need help to progress. Their prayers are answered by more advanced spirits, for "Are they not all ministering spirits, sent forth to minister for them who shall be heirs of salvation?" Hebrews 1:14. This giving of help to lower spirits tends, also, toward the advancement of the higher spirits, who give the help. It is a mutual benefit. "It is more blessed to give than to receive." Acts 20:35.

Spiritualists are firm believers in prayer, — prayer in this life as well as in the next. Dr. Peebles has reported a communication on prayer, of which the following are excerpts:

"Many persons think that it is not permissible to pray, but this we consider a popular delusion amongst those on earth. *We* in spirit life pray for help whenever we want it, let the object be what it may; but not if it is an evil object. In the latter case, prayer is certainly undesirable, for it is the cause of attracting to you spirits who aid you in accomplishing your purpose, perhaps, but they will only increase your unhappiness afterwards; for if you have strong will power you are tempting *them*. On the other hand, if you pray for a good object, you benefit the spirits whom you draw around you. It is good for them to help others; and in helping you, they help themselves. Thus, you see, prayer is a spiritual force which you can put in operation if you have will power enough.

"It is not necessary for a man to pray before he can be helped, but it is advisable; because, although his spirit friends can read his thoughts and understand his wants, he loses the aid of many others who cannot read his thoughts, but who would be attracted to him by his prayers, and would help him if they knew he wanted help. If, however, he never prays, they do not know his needs, and they do not help him. Prayer is, therefore, not merely aspiration, it is something like advertising your wants. All spirits do not see them, it is true; but those who can help you are aware of your needs, and are able to assist you. You should, of course, pray to God, rather than to spirits directly. He permits spirits to execute his decrees. You may not know that this is the case, because you do not see God; but we all live under His laws, and nothing can happen *contrary* to His laws; consequently, whatever is done must be done by Divine sanction, and to Him your prayers should be addressed. We do not say they would be unanswered if addressed to spirits. You can address your prayers to spirits if you like, but it comes to the same thing. You call on the spirit of God — which dwells in their souls as in yours — to help you, and that spirit responds to your call. There is therefore no disgrace in asking help from spirits. *We* do not pray to spirits, but to God. . . . . If the object (prayed for) requires the interference of the highest spirits, you may get it. We do not say that you *will* get it, for, of course, you might pray for impossible things, and we do not say that you will always get what you want in the time that you wish it. You might ask for the immediate conversion of the whole of the spirit world; but this prayer could not be granted without the aid of the Almighty, and therefore you would have to be subject to laws that would necessitate your waiting his time. . . . .

"We have told you of the power of prayer. Now, let us turn to the power of love. The one is the counterpart of the other. Prayer asks, and love grants. If you pray for that which you need, the measure of the love which you are entitled to at the hands of Him you pray to, is evidenced by the response you get to your prayer, be the response favorable or otherwise. If you pray to a human being, the same law applies. If he loves you much, he will respond readily; if not, he refuses. Thus you see that the law is very simple in its application; and in proportion as you merit reward, so will that reward be meted out to you. You will see this law in operation in every phase of life, both in the spiritual and the material worlds. With you its application is of daily occurrence. You refuse the request of your child, not because you don't love it, but because you do. As spirits, we believe in the potency and efficacy of prayer. We know that we grow to be what we aspire to. We delight to pour out our gratitude to the great All-Father, and to pray for assistance from holy ministering angels.

"Matter is moved by spirit. Hence if you hear of matter in the form of clothes, money, and food, being sent to a man in answer to his prayers, as you do in the case of George Muller's Orphanage, at Bristol, where you have one man providing by his will power, or prayers, for the wants of two thousand orphan children, you have a case simply of matter controlled by spirits. . . . . The *modus operandi* we know to be as follows, for we have watched it; the person praying, simply calls to his aid spirits . . . who sympathize with his work; in short, he may be said to advertise for them. The difference between him and others, who solicit your charitable contributions, is that he advertises in the spiritual world. We have called it advertising, simply to convey an idea to your mind that you can comprehend, but in reality it is nothing of the kind; it is an earnest appeal by spirit power to those whose necessities require that they should lend help of this kind. Hence you see it is a mutual benefit. 'It is more blessed to give than to receive'."

What the *ultimate* goal of this progression is, the communicating spirits do not tell, for the reason, admittedly, that they do not know. They believe, however, that as they progress, they are constantly approaching nearer to Godlikeness. The prevailing opinion is that expressed as follows by an English physician who had been in spirit life for forty-eight years, and had died at the age of thirty-five:

"The human soul never ceases to progress through all eternity, rising to ever higher and higher states of beatitude, becoming more and more *at one* with the Father, until it is all Divine and like unto God."

The spirits urge us to commence our progression here and now. They say we can make more progress with less effort now than after death. The way to progress, here and hereafter, is to discard all delusions of grandeur and, in all humility, to serve those in need of help.

Spiritualists believe that Heaven and hell are not places, but are conditions of happiness or unhappiness within one's self; and that as one progresses, one partakes more of Heaven, be it here or hereafter. As Jesus said, "Neither shall they say, Lo here! or, Lo there! for, behold, the kingdom of God is within you." Luke 17:21.

The departed teach us, as Dr. Peebles has so well written, "that *memory is a recording angel*—that the moral cowardice we have been guilty of, the false pretenses that we have hidden behind, the selfish motives that have guided, the vile passions not resisted, the scheming motives that have ruled our conduct, will all meet us in judgment array in the land of soul-revelation, where masks are of no avail, and all—*all* these memories will there torture until the uttermost farthing has been paid, and due restitution made.

"They teach, on the other hand, that every kind word spoken, every generous deed done, every wise sympathy extended, every truth vindicated, every pure principle woven into their life-garment, as well as every mortal whom we have done good unto, will be there in vivid realities to gladden our souls, and make more radiant our pathway."

The following are a few of the things which Dr. Beecher, of Barkhamsted, Conn., communicated after his transition.

"I was ill but a few days—dying suddenly. As I now look back, the event was but a shock—a momentary loss of consciousness. I could hardly believe at first that I had died, as I was still in the familiar apartment. That a change had come over me, however, was certain; and yet I could not comprehend it. I never felt more alive; and still I could not seem to exactly adjust myself to the new conditions of being. When mortals come into the earthly life, there are those expecting them—those who have made preparation for their reception; so, with the higher birth, my father met me. I was clothed; (and) almost immediately my (deceased) wife and daughter approached me. This for the moment added to my confusion. These all extended hands of welcome, but I could not readily speak. Others, whom I had known in the body, came to me, awakening memories of by-gone years. . . . Casting my eyes towards earthly friends weeping over the mortal remains that I had left, I thought I would make myself known to them that they might understand that death was only transition—the new and better birth; but I could neither make them see or hear me. It was a sad disappointment. I was thoroughly myself—an individual man with consciousness, reason, and memory of wordly experiences. . . . At first my father was my teacher; . . . My father brought to me a spirit guide (ministering spirit) far in advance of me. His presence was commanding and his lessons divine. I looked up to him with reverence, and his teachings thrilled me with ecstacy. . . . Mortals entering spirit life are but little more than children. . . . I had not been long in this world of spirits before I was taken to the temple of self-examination, and left alone. The silence was almost painful. My memory seemed unaccountably vivid. My earthly life passed before me like a panorama. I seemed to see everything, especially *myself*. My very being was a glass. Not only my acts, but my motives seemed to rise up before me. It was the judgment, and yet a judgment tempered with mercy. For while bewailing the past, my guide came, bidding me look, not upon the past, but to press upward and on in the golden future."

Aaron Knight, after he had been in the spirit world for almost two hundred years, communicated,

"Many persons in spirit-life, when they look back upon their earthly existence, see in it so much that is weak and childish, if not positively revolting, that they do not desire others to look upon it. But the time comes to all human souls when it is necessary for them to unveil all their earth-life to the clear light of the spirit-world about them, for by so doing they put themselves in accord with their surroundings. Unity cannot exist where there is deception, or hiding of any past conditions of life."

The deceased Mr. Scott was in the light. As reported in "From Four who are Dead," he communicated, "We do not grow old, but remain always young and strong. Our bodies are solid,"—to his perception—"as solid as yours, but different. . . . We are making a new world here, a world of assorted types, men and women who can contribute to its efficiency, and who are willing to produce the sort of results we want. You see, we do not want a repetition of the muddles of our earth life, and we are left to our own devices to produce what we think best." Asked whether people who persistently cheated people in earth life still continue to do the same on the other side, he replied, "They will be the same, but they will learn the folly of indulging in their evil ways. People tend to improve, also there are not the same temptations here. We have no possessions, and there is no competition, and no hunger—as we do not eat. And no sex jealousy, as sex with us is not physical. It is an attraction, it is love, but not greedy possession. I love you, but I don't want you only for myself. I want your happiness, and am content whatever you may choose to do. . . . People are coming over all the time and everywhere. They step into this world, and stand about looking puzzled. Then I — or someone else, for there are lots of us doing this—go up to them and accost them. You can't think how bewildered they are at first. It is so different from what they expect. We are differently constituted, and our serenity is part of our make-up. Fussing, fidgeting and fretting are unknown here — no — *it isn't dull.* Work with us is not the same as work with you. It is not physical. *It is thought.* We decide on what must be done, and the decision is all that is necessary." "We are not material in the sense that you are, but our bodies appear to be solid. . . . We . . . resemble our earthly forms at our best; perhaps we improve on them a bit. I am better looking than I was, and yet if you saw me you would recognize me." Asked whether they lived in houses, he replied, "We do not need shelters, but we like to have a place that we can look on as ours, a place to return to and rest in. . . . It is not ours in the sense of being a possession; it is more a place with which we are familiar and which we like. . . . Our world is here, there and everywhere. It is a matter of vibration . . . a vibration they do not know about yet. This is a bigger world than yours and a far brighter one. As nobody looks old or infirm, it is difficult to tell how long they have been here." . . . "I told you that they have decided it would be good for you and for us that we should establish communion with your world. We are trying to do it. We do it fumblingly. We are not as yet very highly developed, and therefore our opinions are not yet of much value."

It should be realized, however, that spirits in darkness, and spirits in greater light than Mr. Scott, find themselves existing under conditions differing from his. Consequently, their descriptions naturally differ somewhat from his given above.

It is a great mistake to suppose, as some do, that spirits are omniscient. There are many differences of opinion there, as here. Sometimes an opinionated spirit will communicate, as a fact, a thing which is merely his opinion, but which he nevertheless believes to be true. There are even differences of opinion there, as here, on the doctrine of the Trinity, and the precise nature of Jesus. Opinionated spirits may contradict one another on this question and on other points on which they are not correctly informed.

The earth is full of fools, jokers, liars and deceitful persons. Since their characters do not change immediately upon death, the other side contains many such unprogressed spirits who seek opportunities to communicate deliberate falsehoods and lies. Persons receiving communications must be on their guard against them. Hence the Biblical warning, mentioned above, "Beloved, believe not every spirit, but try the spirits whether they are of God."

The beliefs of Spiritualists are based on an enormous number of communications, received during the centuries, from which the wheat of agreement has been sifted from the chaff of disagreement.

It is the belief of Spiritualists that the *Divine Law* has never been better stated than by Jesus, when he said,

"Thou shalt love the Lord thy God with all thy heart, and with all thy soul, and with all thy mind. This is the first and great commandment. And the second is like unto it. Thou shalt love thy neighbor as thyself. On these two commandments hang all the law and the prophets." Mat. 22:37-40.

Spiritualists believe that the better we are able, here and hereafter, to comply with these two commandments, the faster we progress and grow toward Godlikeness.

ALL IS LIFE

By HENRY KNIGHTON

Send forth the song of Truth,
Let joyous news take wing,
Proclaim to age and youth
That death has lost its sting.
The dread and fearful foe
Has gone with yesterday,
For Truth has dealt the blow,
And death means life today.

Refrain:

So banish fear and dread,
All is life, There are no dead.

The voices from on high
Proclaim in accents clear,
"We live and do not die,
We watch and bring you cheer;
For all is life and love
And there's no death to fear;
We're near, yes just above,
Tune in and you will hear.

Let every one arise
And help a grieving soul
To see, as do the wise,
That death is not the goal.
We'll tell of God's great plan
To cast out fear and strife;
How angels say to man,
That death just brings new life.

The music of this official hymn of the General Assembly of Spiritualists may be found on Page 1 of the General Assembly Hymnal.

THERE'S JOY O MY SOUL

By REV. CONVERSE E. NICKERSON

There's joy, O my soul, in the song of His love,
There's comfort and healing and balm;
For Love's sun is shining eternal above
And shedding its infinite calm.
Though pathways are stony and dreary to tread,
And thorns spring so oft from the sod,
The path leads to beauty and smiles just ahead,
For onward and upward is God.

The birds praise His wisdom with carols of trust,
The stars give a token of might,
While time brings the witness that His ways are just,
Forever to live in His light.
My soul, lift thine eyes from the darkness of dust
To see thy great Master's command;
Repose with a simple and implicit trust
Thy ways to His loving strong hand.

O sing with the morning its paean of joy,
And cheerful thy long day shall be;
A prayer in thine heart every fear shall destroy,
Thou strength for thy journey shall see.
Thy soul is His image, unquenchable flame,
Thy task is His glory to show;
Thy song is His law, given forth in His name,
Complete in His likeness to grow.

The music of this hymn may be found on Page 14 of the General Assembly Hymnal.

FACT OR FICTION

By Mrs. St. Clair-Storart

SPIRITUALISM is either fact or fiction.

If communion with the Beyond is impossible today, it has always been impossible.

In that case, first of all we must relegate the religion of Jesus to the region of fairy tales, for if communion with spirits is impossible, then Jesus was either Himself deliberately deceiving the world, or He was Himself deceived, or alternately the whole story of the Gospels is a fake or an invention, and in this case the Christian religion, which is to-day avowed by countless millions of human beings, was founded on the biggest lie in the records of mankind. For no fair-minded person can dispute the fact that communion with spirits was the basis and the continuous accompaniment of the life of Jesus as recorded in the Bible. His very birth was preceded by visitations of spirits to Joseph and Mary. Also the shepherds knew of His birth through the agency of spirit beings.

Again, it was through a warning given by a spirit to Joseph and by his fleeing into Egypt, that the life of the infant Jesus was saved. From Matt. xv., 27, it would seem certain that Jesus was in the habit of teaching His disciples at what we to-day call seances, for He says to them, "What I tell you in the darkness" (that is presumably of the seance room) "speak ye in the light, and what ye hear in the ear" (by the direct voice of the spirit during these sittings) "proclaim upon the house-tops."

Again, what meaning is there in the episode of the Transfiguration if there is not and never has been communion with those who have passed? And what of the Resurrection and the subsequent appearances? These constitute for Christians the most vital portion of the Bible.

If communion with the dead is and has always been impossible, then Jesus did not appear to the women and to His disciples, and the whole Christian religion crumbles into nothingness, and, with it, everything else of value in the world.

Again, what of the religion of the Jews? We have ample justification for asserting that Moses' whole life's mission and his teachings were from first to last directed by spirits, from the episode of the so-called burning bush, when he received instructions by direct voice as to his great work in the future, to the final warning as to the manner and reason of his approaching death. Communion with the spirit world was the controlling factor in his every-day life. The Ten Commandments were given to him by spirit writing on tablets of stone. His instructions for the building of the Tabernacle were conveyed by what is to-day called the "direct voice" of a spirit.

If therefore, communion to and from the spirit world is and has always been impossible, then, if Moses existed as an historic figure, either he was a gross deceiver and conducted the exodus and founded the Jewish religion upon a gigantic bluff, or the whole story is a faked fairy tale which has successfully deceived millions of sincere and intellectual people of all ages and nationalities. And what we have said concerning the religions of Jesus and Moses applies with equal force to the religion of all great religious leaders, for these teachers were inspired to their missions by direct commands from spirits and from them they derived their confidence to go forth and preach their gospels to the world.

Therefore if Spiritualism is fiction, fake or fraud, then all the great religions of the world were founded upon fiction, fake or fraud. And thus if it is true that we owe the bulk of our civilization—along its moral and its spiritual lines—to the religions of the world, we are driven to the absurd corollary that the moral and spiritual evolution mankind has been founded upon fake or fraud. A rather ignoble origin for such munificent result.

If Spiritualism is fiction, life on this earth is a funeral procession leading only to the tomb, its route bordered by the gravestones of loved ones who have preceded us in the funeral cortege. Of what use the gradual evolution of our human consciousness, if the only Truth of which we are to become conscious is annihilation after protracted sufferings? But, thank God, we Spiritualists know from personal experience that there is a future life, that this life is a spirit life, and that man can, here on this earth communicate with that life. We know, in short, that Spiritualism is not fiction, it is fact.

If Spiritualism is fact, then this life is not a funeral procession, it is a triumphant journey towards a clearly defined goal. God has taken care to afford us, through special messengers, opportunities of learning the laws concerning a future life and the conditions in which on this earth we can best prepare for the life of spirit which is to come.

We Spiritualists draw our facts of survival at first hand; for us there is no such thing as death, and though nothing, not even Spiritualism, can compensate us for the personal loss when the physical parting comes, the sting of death has gone, for we know that our beloved is living more gloriously than we and that communion is not necessarily severed. For ourselves the fear of death is transmuted almost into a hope; death in any of its forms is but the turnstile leading into everlasting life. We are no longer merely sojourners on an evanescent earth, we are the legatees of a greater inheritance, literally joint-heirs with God and inheritors of the Kingdom of Heaven.

THE MESSAGE OF SPIRITUALISM

By FLORENCE AYLING

The religion of Spiritualism has a message for the world. It is true that there are many people who are not ready to accept the material and spiritual help that it brings to mankind or to avail themselves of the consolation brought to those bereaved of their loved ones.

We are not at this time referring to the personal messages received through mediums from the ones who have "gone over" to what we call the Spirit World. These are, indeed, wonderful and (to us) sacred and certainly do prove the continuity of life.

First (and this is the A. B. C. of spiritual growth) it teaches that a person *never dies.* One only changes the body from the physical to the spiritual. Each individual has two bodies, you know. Refer to 1st Corinthians, the 15th chapter, the 44th verse in which Paul tells us of this. Then after we make the transition from the physical to the spiritual, we meet our loved ones, go to the home we have earned for ourselves and go right on living.

When death of the physical body occurs, the next step depends upon the individual circumstances and what kind of a life the person in mention has led while here. For instance, if a person has been ill for a long time and is mentally and physically tired, he will be allowed to sleep, watched over by the guides and loved ones until he awakens naturally and is then taken to his spiritual home.

Often death occurs quickly and the individual arrives in the Spirit World in a hurry, so to speak. To say they are bewildered is putting the case mildly, but after receiving help from those who are there, most of them become resigned to being "dead" as regards their earth life and are ready to "carry-on" where they find themselves.

In the case of a small child, it is received into the Spirit World by loving hands and taken to a beautiful place where it is tenderly cared for and taught, where it grows each day in beauty and wisdom.

We carry our personalities with us, our characteristics and the love we have in our hearts for others. This love will impel us to visit those whom we have left on the earth, and God gives us the privilege of coming back to them, watching over and helping even though they are (most of the time at least) totally unaware of our presence.

Spiritualism teaches us that we are governed by spiritual as well as material laws. A knowledge or even a partial knowledge of this beautiful Truth, taught by the Philosophy of Spiritualism will take from all mankind the fear of Death and be of great consolation when we are parted from our dear ones by the death of their physical bodies. We say *consolation* because there is no power to take from our consciousness the heavy veil of mourning and sorrow that comes to us in the "passing over" of one whom we love, but the knowledge that he or she has gone on before us, still loves us and comes back to us— that the world beyond is more beautiful than this one (if we have lived rightly)—makes life easier then. All this will comfort us and the black mourning veil will lift much more quickly than in the case of a materially-minded person.

Our spiritual bodies are perfect. We leave all defects behind and who knows but that many a person "going over" has been glad to leave behind a pair of eyes that were sightless or some other physical affliction?

INVOCATION AND SERMONETTE No. 1

Invocation:

Unto Thee, Infinite Spirit of Wisdom, Truth, and Love, we lift our hearts this day. Give unto us a broader vision of Thy great providence that covers all things. Open our spiritual eyes that we may behold the truth of Thy spiritual world: may its healing harmonies soften our earthly distresses and bring us rest. Help us to know that all about us are the Everlasting Arms of Thy Love. So may we learn the lesson it teaches and adjust ourselves to its environment of understanding. Come in unto us, great Infinite Spirit, and draw us nearer to Thyself, Our Heavenly Father.

Sermonette: "The Spiritual World"

We invite your attention to a subject which must interest every one who believes in the possibility of a life after this, and of another world in which we are to dwell forever. How can an intelligent being remain indifferent to a subject of such infinite importance, if he believes in its reality? We see, one after another of those whom we know and love passing away; we know that we must follow them. How then, can a rational being be indifferent to the consideration of that other world, its nature and the condition of its inhabitants?

What is Spirit? What is Matter? These are primary questions, 'tis true, but most important. Upon the correct answer to them must depend all distinct and true knowledge concerning the spiritual world.

We believe that spirit is substance, and must have a form. There are material substances and spiritual substances, entirely distinct from each other.

Every material thing is made out of some material substance. The earth itself is formed out of a former gaseous substance. The material body is formed and organized of material substances of various kinds.

In the same sense we mean that spirit is a substance, and that every spiritual essence is formed from some spiritual substance. All Christian philosophy acknowledges that angels are spirits; if they are, they are formed of spiritual substances. If there is a spiritual world distinct from the material world, that world and all the things in it must be formed of spiritual substances. If we are asked what a spiritual substance is *in itself*, we cannot tell. It is just as impossible, however, to form any idea of what a material substance is in itself. Who can tell what clay, or wood, or iron, or water, or gas, is in itself? Our knowledge of everything is limited by its relations to us; by its effects upon us. We are no more called upon to define what spirit is in itself than we are to define what matter is in itself. It is impossible to do either.

If there is any such existence, or being, or entity, as a spirit, it must have substance and form. It is impossible for the mind to conceive of anything without form. Spirit as well as matter, must therefore have substance and form, for they are two factors which are essential to any existence, or to the conception of any being or thing. Spirit is the correlative, not the negation of matter.

Paul declares:

"There is a natural body, and there is a spiritual body.

Howbeit that was not first which is spiritual, but that which is natural; and afterward that which is spiritual."

—1st Cor. 15: 44, 46.

We have the natural body now,—of material substance. Afterward we shall have the spiritual body,—of spiritual substance.

Benediction:

Our thanks to Thee, O Father, for the privilege of the exercise of Reason. We bless Thee that Thou hast performed all things for our good; that Knowledge and Understanding may be ours if we will to seek them. To Thee be all honor and glory. Amen.

REVELATION

Say not that death is king, that night is lord,
That loveliness is passing, beauty dies;
Nor tell me hope's a vain, deceptive dream
Fate lends to life, a pleasing, luring gleam
To light awhile the earth's despondent skies,
Till Death brings swift and sure its dread reward.
Say not that youth deceives, but age is true,
That roses quickly pass, while cypress bides,
That happiness is foolish, grief is wise,
That stubborn dust shall choke our human cries.
Death tells new worlds, and life immortal hides
Beyond the veil, which shall all wrongs undo.
This was the tale God breathed to me at dawn
When flooding sunrise told that night was gone.

—*Thomas Curtis Clark*

INVOCATION AND SERMONETTE No. 2

Invocation:

O Spirit of Infinite Truth, we thank Thee this day for the light of Thy power throughout the ages. Hope has led us along that path of Thy radiance. By Thy light we have witnessed the true glory of God. The comfort of Thy presence has bidden us lay aside our fears and walk forward trusting in the sureness of Thy leadership. Into the presence of angels have we been ushered to find that glad reunion of spirit which testifies to the great Family and kinship of which we are an immortal part. Keep us steadfast in the resolve to know more of Thee, that through Thee we may come to know God. Amen.

Sermonette, "The Light of Life"

William Shakespeare, who wrote so illuminatingly on all conditions of men, and the thoughts of men, gave us the mortal picture of this life we live on earth. Here in the frame of his matchless description and music, we see our mortal selves:

"Our revels now are ended. These our actors
Are melted into air, into thin air;
And, like the baseless fabric of this vision,
The cloud capped towers, the gorgeous palaces,
The solemn temples, the great globe itself,
Yes, all which it inherits, shall dissolve,
And, like this insubstantial pageant faded,
Leave not a rack behind. We are such stuff
As dreams are made on, and our little life
Is rounded with a sleep."

What made these "our revels" so full of joy and light? Was it not the eternal spirit of the living soul? Was it not the great light of intelligence that animated the scene and kept it vibrant with color, and joy and endeavor? When this light steps away, naturally, all the trappings or earthly array must fade and dissolve,—melt into thin air.

It were a hopelessly dreary waste, if the whole meaning of our activity upon this stage of earth were finality and death. Meaningless chaos would be the inscription left upon the ruin. All the purpose of creation would become unintelligible and whatever philosophy of hope that man now possesses would perish.

Since all things of the material must fade and fall, including man's mortal existence, then there is no hope but that of immortality. "There is a spirit in man," and that spirit is the Light of Life! It is the divinely lighted candle that death and dissolution cannot extinguish. What a sublime thought,—our spirits are divinely lighted, never to become extinguished.

The God that made all things in creation, has made also an eternal country, invisible to the eyes of mortality, but bright and gloriously visible to the eyes of spirit. "In my Father's house are many mansions,—if it were not so I would have told you," saith the inspired and divine prophet.

Benediction:

Love Eternal mantle us round about that we keep safe with thee. Divine guardian of life and affection, dissolve our doubts and our fears by the pervading spirit of God. Amen.

EACH DAY IS NEW

Each day is new. Bear that in mind.
    Wipe off the old day's slate,
And turn with zest to meet the tasks
    That in the new day wait.
This is a shining motto set:
    Forget the yesterdays'
Mistakes, remember but their joy,
    Their kind deeds and their praise.
Upon the substance of the joys
    You knew in times gone by
Build this new day and let its goal
    Swing beautiful and high.
Each day is new. It waits your will,
    Go forth to it and say,
"With courage and new faith and hope
    I'll turn to this new day."

—*George Elliston*

INVOCATION AND SERMONETTE No. 3

Invocation:

Our Heavenly Father, in Thee we live and move and have our true being. In the great ocean of Thy Mind do we exist and from Thee do we obtain every gift and blessing. To-day we come close to that fount of power asking that Thou wilt send Thy holy messengers of Love and Instruction to bring us nearer unto Thee. May our loved ones be close to us this day, shedding their spiritual radiance upon us and infusing strength where there is weakness; courage where there is fear; comfort where there is sorrow; and peace where there is restlessness. To Thee be our thanks and adoration. Amen.

Sermonette: "True Religion"

"A correct understanding of God constitutes true religion." This we voice in our Principles of Spiritualism.

. Progress in any line of endeavor comes from understanding and practice. Instruction has been the rule all through our lives, from infancy up. To be taught correctly is the important thing. Our habits of thought and action spring from the instruction we have received. The heathen, wrongly and superstitiously taught, forms habits which hold him back and deny him the progress of the foremost nations of the earth. The wicked person has fallen into such wickedness because of ignorance and idleness.

To learn the Perfect Way is the objective of all systems of enlightened religion. That perfect way must lead toward God. That perfect way must be along the paths of Truth. "Whatsoever things that are true," counselled Paul.

Jesus promised "Ye shall know the truth, and the truth shall make you free." He was telling mankind that progress would be gained from knowing the truth. Ignorance ever is an obstruction to progress.

In the sincere efforts to learn what is true we must search our hearts and determine that we shall not be swerved from accepting truth when we find it; regardless of what our friends may say of us, if truth in religion means to experience knowledge of a spirit world, and its ministers of communication, we will bravely accept.

To know God aright is to recognize that truth.

The living of a righteous life on earth for just ourselves is a selfish thing; but righteousness practiced for the reason that it fits us to live in a better manner among those about us, is worthy of the highest principles of religion. Our progressive betterment here in this world is for the divine purpose of being ready for entrance in a higher sphere of expression, which is the spirit world. Hence righteous living is but gaining spiritual instruction for a better life beyond this.

The practice of "true religion" means all of this.

Then can we join the poet in his song when he sings:

"Through Love to Light! Oh, wonderful the way
That leads from darkness to the perfect day;
From darkness and from dolor of the night
To morning that comes singing o'er the sea!
Through Love to Light! Through Light, O God, to Thee,
Who art the Love of love, the Eternal Light of light!"

Benediction:

May the light of Truth light our way. May its beams bring trust and understanding. Through our inner consciousness may we gain the great at-one-ment with Infinite Intelligence. Amen.

INVOCATION AND SERMONETTE No. 4

Invocation:

Dear Father God, we come in thankfulness to Thee for the opportunity for praise and prayer. That inbreathing of Thy Spirit we need that its quickening power may increase our yearning after Thee. In the safe refuge of Thy tender Love we seek to know Thee better. Coming unto Thee we find rest and the divine refreshment of soul which alone can beget for us spiritual vision. Our trust is in Thee, O Father. Looking toward that day-dawn when we shall dwell more fully in Thy presence with those who have loved us on earth and with whom we long for companionship, we rest in the confidence of Thy Spirit this day. May their love and Thy Commandments inspire us toward greater service in Thy Name. Amen.

Sermonette: "Prayer"

One of his disciples said unto him, "Lord, teach us to pray."
And Jesus answered:
After this manner, therefore, pray ye:
Our Father which art in heaven,
    Our Eternal Father, Pervading Spiritual Love,
Hallowed by Thy name,
    Forever honored, forever blessed, forever loved,
Thy kingdom come,
    Hasten the complete harmony of Thy will,
Thy will be done in earth, as it is in heaven,
    May Thy Infinite Mind and Spirit be in all the earth among men,
Give us this day our daily bread,
    Give us of Thy grace and spiritually sustain us,
And forgive us our debts, as we forgive our debtors,
    Make us worthy of Thy love through justice and compassion,
And lead us not into temptation, but deliver us from evil,
    Lead us out of temptation, guard us from evil,
For Thine is the kingdom, and the power, and the glory, forever.
    Thou art infinite, all-loving, all-merciful, Love, Truth, and Life Perpetual.
Prayer is the soul's sincere desire.
Jesus said "When thou prayest, enter into thy closet, and when thou hast shut the door, pray to thy Father which is in secret, and thy

Father which seeth in secret shall reward thee openly. Your Father knoweth what ye have need of, before ye ask Him."

Mortal bodies cry out in pain, or weariness, or thirst: only the spirit prays. In the atmosphere of prayer we approach spiritual things. There, in the purity of the spirit we can shut ourselves away from the roughness and the inharmony, the doubtings and confusions of the flesh. In the anteroom of the subconscious we can touch the mighty forces of spiritual power and find them transmuted into fruitful harvest in our daily lives.

Prayer is thus the divinely designed avenue through which we replenish our spiritual strength and vision.

When we pray we lift the spiritual within us to become the dominant self,—into its rightful and natural place. When it is in control all things are harmonious. Just as "thoughts are things," so prayer, rightly prayed, transforms, heals and renews.

The Master counseled. "Men ought always to pray, and not to faint."

Benediction:

Dear loved in spirit, teach us to pray. And as we go from hence let the atmosphere of sincere prayer go with us. Impress us with the desire for good-will, harmony and love. Give us joy and peace that we may commune with thee. So may we grow in spiritual worth and goodness. Amen.

"PRAYER"

These are the gifts I ask of thee, Spirit serene—
Strength for the daily task;
Courage to face the road;
Good cheer to help me bear the traveller's load;
And for the hours of rest that come between,
And inward joy in all things heard and seen.
These are the sins I fain would have thee take away—
Malice and cold disdain;
Hot anger, sullen hate;
Scorn of the lowly, envy of the great;
And discontent that casts a shadow gray
On all the brightness of a common day.

—*Henry VanDyke*

Pray for my soul. More things are wrought by prayer
Than this world dreams of. Wherefore let thy voice
Rise like a fountain for me night and day.
For what are men better than sheep or goats
That nourish a blind life within the brain
If, knowing God they lift not hands of prayer
Both for themselves and those who call them friends?
For so the whole round earth is every way
Bound by gold chains about the feet of God.

—Alfred Tennyson

INVOCATION AND SERMONETTE No. 5

Invocation:

O Spirit of Divine Harmony, Wisdom and Love. Again we come before the altar of Truth and beseech Thy blessing. Array us in spiritual garments of peace. Make Love our staff and let us put on the sandals of Courage that we may faithfully walk in Thy pathways. We pray for the power to see the right road to spiritual progression. Let us tune ourselves to the Divine Harmonies of the Soul, that we may catch the sound of the heavenly strain and strengthen ourselves in the fullness of its vibrations. Help us to learn the laws of spiritual health, and to cast from us weak temptation of misunderstanding and darkness. In Thee do we praise Our Heavenly Father for all His love and care over us. Amen.

Sermonette: "Divine Harmonies"

"How sweet the moonlight sleeps upon this bank!
Here will we sit and let the sounds of music
Creep in our ears: soft stillness and the night
Become the touches of sweet harmony.
. . . Look how the floor of heaven
Is thick inlaid with patines of bright gold;
There's not the smallest orb which thou beholdest
But in his motion like an angel sings,—
Such harmony is in immortal souls;
But whilst this muddy vesture of decay
Doth grossly close it in, we cannot hear it."

Thus Shakespeare tells us of the celestial harmonies which the soul could be conscious of if it were not for material things. Man, while on earth, is of two natures,—mortal and immortal. His sicknesses,—inharmonies,—are really caused by this unattunement. Striving always to live, and yet blindly, he often fails to learn wisdom and understanding. A peace of mind could produce that harmony within which brings perfect health. To have perfect spiritual control means complete health and happiness.

There is harmony in the true courses of Nature and poets have sung of the sweet "music of the spheres". There is harmony of the forces and laws of the spirit; we only need to find that harmony. The knowledge of spiritual truth can put it within our grasp and practice. When Jesus healed the sick and He restored that harmony by the psychic powers which He possessed. He taught that spiritual power could heal the sick; could bring happiness; could fulfill the prayer which asks "Thy will be done on earth, as it is done in heaven." This meant in very truth that spiritual harmony was the working of the will of God.

As we know that fear brings nervous destruction and other ills, so we know that confidence of mind brings health. Confidence of mind is also spiritual power. The spirit within is the only force that can exercise such power. Then if we WILL to be well, we can do much toward becoming so. "Such harmony is in immortal souls." When Jesus declared "Thy faith hath made thee whole," he meant that spiritual power was again in control, casting out fear and inharmony and disease.

Benediction:

May the peace which passeth understanding, rest and abide with us, delivering us from evil, blessing us with health, and confirming us in everlasting Love. Amen.

"And He came down with them, and stood in the plain, and the company of His disciples, and a great multitude of people out of all Judea and Jerusalem, came to hear Him, and to be healed of their diseases;

And they that were vexed with unclean spirits: and they were healed.

And the multitude sought to touch Him: for there went virtue out of Him, and healed them all."

—Luke 6:17, 18, 19.

INVOCATION AND SERMONETTE No. 6

Easter

Invocation:

Great Guiding Force from Realms Eternal, we are privileged in communing in sacred fellowship under the radiant power of Thy Divine Mind. Grant to us this hour the revelation of Thy Spirit of Truth. Send upon us the healing beams of Thy Love and Assurance. Continue within us the courage and inspiration which came in that morningtime of our conversion to the knowledge of the truth of immortality as revealing in our religion of Spiritualism. May the nearness of the beautiful Summerland keep our ambitious zeal aflame that we may be living examples of spiritual faith and workers of righteousness. Amen.

Paul declared: "If Christ be not risen, then is our preaching vain and your faith is also vain."

The resurrection of Jesus, as Paul preached it, was the objective affirmation that there is no death. Jesus risen from the realms of the dead meant the continuation of His message to His disciples, and the definite confirmation of everything He had promised them about His Father's kingdom of eternal life.

When He had affirmed to them, "Ye should be glad that I go unto the Father, for the Father is greater than I," He was comforting them in the most positive way, for hereby He said, "Because I live, ye shall live also."

They could not understand that He meant that his invisible spirit would go into heaven, for they looked for Him to remain as their leader upon the earth; some of them even thought that physically He could not see death. Death to them was a mystery and a closing of the door of life. Only some days after His death upon the cross did they realize that He indeed lived in the kingdom of spirit. Such a heartening realization inspired them to go forward and preach His gospel; yea, even to go onward through martyrdom, still praising God and smilingly passing through death to eternal existence, into his Father's kingdom; even as Jesus had preceded them.

Paul had written of death, "When this corruptible shall have put on incorruption, then shall be brought to pass the saying, 'Death where is thy sting, O Grave, where is thy victory?'"

The saying is still mysterious, and in some points of interpretation dark and unsolved. We do understand, at least, that incorruption is equivalent to immortality. The process of gaining immortality of substance is a scientific one. It is an inheritance of God through the laws of His spiritual creation. Its substance is a clothing of the spiritual garment upon the soul at the point of its departure from the mortal and corruptible body. It is the exchanging of the living garment for that of death.

Man lives in the midst of eternity, and his destined experiences constrain him to travel from birth to transition, and then on through more wondrous and countless experiences in the spirit world. Paul has used the phrase, "Changed from glory into glory."

Thus, earthly life is but a moment of time.

The last words of one of our American Presidents were: "This is the last of earth."

Edwin Booth, the great American actor, made this statement of faith in the life hereafter:

"A light from heaven has settled in my soul, and I regard death, as God intended we should understand it, as the breaking of eternal daylight and a birthday of the soul."

Great was the joy of Mary, the mother of Jesus, when she saw her son spiritually raised, standing before her. Only the truth of our spiritual philosophy of life after death can make possible our acceptance of this fact concerning Jesus of Nazareth. If His teaching and experience are true, then indeed is Spiritualism's religion a truth, and we hold the key to the mystery of Death.

The Easter session is the symbol and the sign of Light and Truth, —"To them which sat in the Valley and the Shadow of Death, New Light is sprung up."

INVOCATION AND SERMONETTE No. 7

Christmas

Invocation:

O Spirit of Infinite Light, this Christmastide we lift our hearts unto Thee and ask that in us may truly shine the Christmas light. May it reflect Thy great glory, and soften round about us all discord and dimness of spiritual vision. Bring to our hearthstone the quiet peace that surrounded the Babe of Bethlehem. Gird us round about with spiritual strength and courage. We give Thee praise and thanks for the Light of Christmas; its glow and blessing warm us in the reflection of Thy great eternal Love. O enlarge our spirit of gratefulness and give unto us the understanding that will brighten our pathway. In the knowledge of the comfort that there is no death we rest in safety. Let the ray of Thy countenance shine upon us this day. In humbleness and sincerity we ask it. Amen.

Reading:

"And there were in the same country shepherds abiding in the field, keeping watch over their flock by night.

And lo, the angel of the Lord came upon them, and the glory of the Lord shone round about them; and they were sore afraid.

And the angel said unto them, Fear not: for, behold, I bring you tidings of great joy, which shall be to all people.

And suddenly there was with the angel a multitude of the heavenly host, praising God, and saying,

Glory to God in the highest, and on earth peace, good will toward
men."   —Luke, 2:8 to 14.

One of the impressive thoughts which the Christmas picture brings to us is that of the Three Wise Men who brought gifts to the Christ-child. It suggests to us the Divine truth that Jesus, the great spiritual teacher, was a perfect gift of God to humanity; his teachings were to show the way to righteousness and Divine Love; his examples was the pattern of perfection which God has designed for each of us.

These great Eastern sages were so grateful, knowing that here was a spiritual light that would bring the knowledge of immortality to the world, that they celebrated their joy by the presentation of costly gifts.

We do also commemorate the birth of Jesus in this festival of good will, by making it a gift day for our dear ones. The Christmas tree represents a symbol of our "tree of loving hearts" as we joyously sing and give thanks to God for His perfect expressions of Love.

Also we would remember that at the occasion of the lowly manger birth of Mary's son, there was revealed the brilliant and glorious presence of the angel hosts, praising God and joyfully singing of peace and love. The shepherds' hearts glowed within them at the sudden and beautiful revelation.

"Peace on earth, good will toward men,"—the dream of perfect union with the will of Divine Love. Not yet fully realized on earth among men, but still inspiring the hearts of all mankind who today contemplate this great celestial advent of the heavenly host. From the exalted realms of Light they came. Their message has never ceased through the centuries to enflame our hearts with joy. How beautiful must be that spiritual region where they dwell! How perfect the happiness they know there!

Our Spiritualism points our way to that blessed region, not as some fanciful dream, but as a living truth to which we shall finally attain.

The Christmas message is therefore a vital one. When we would be discouraged and think we are desolate and isolated in this vale of dust and mortality, let us realize that a great light shone round about the shepherds that night on the Judean hills; in the atmosphere of that Light were the exalted ones from the spirit world. Too, our dear beloved ones who have passed on are there now; they draw very near to us and seek to cheer us; their presence revives in us the inspiration of spiritual truth, that we may look to the everlasting heights and praise God for Life and Immortality.

Jesus said, "Let not your hearts be troubled; in my Father's house are many mansions." It was one of his great messages to us; because of it we worship in joy and cheerfulness at his shrine this Christmas day.

Love is the central message of Jesus and his followers,—Love that interprets for us the true likeness of God the Father. Such love in our hearts is strong enough to cast out fear, and sin, and distrust. Such love will make understanding hearts and clear vision, so that in time we shall come to "love our neighbor as ourselves."

Good will is centered in such a love. Its bright Star shines on leading us ever upward. We cannot know God without perfect love; we cannot be spiritually conditioned to live in that perfect sphere of joy in the after-life without the knowledge of Divine Love. The kingdom of heaven is within us as we absorb its essence and its power. To do so is to become divine and to enter into the fullness of the Kingdom of Spirit.

These are some of the thoughts that Christmas inspires. We have a right to worship spiritual truth in the form of Jesus, the manger babe; it was his purity and spiritual perfection that led the world through a time when humanity was treading its darkest pathway.

"The day spring from on high hath visited us,
To give light to them which sit in darkness and in the shadow of death, to guide our feet into the way of peace."

—Luke, 1:78, 79.

INVOCATION AND SERMONETTE No. 8

Memorial Service

Invocation:

Divine Master of Life, O Eternal God, we come before Thee this day in humble consecration. We would remember at this hour the loves and friendships of those dear to us who have crossed to that divine existence of immortality. In their names we consecrate this hour; in their memories we invoke the blessing of Divine Love. Make us pure within, O God, as we draw close to that sweet atmosphere of memory; in it we have enshrined those dear ones who once walked the earth pathway with us. May the recollection of their smiles and firm words of inspiring courage renew in us a spiritual resolve, bringing our hearts unto unison with Thee. Love that binds us together in one family circle unites and draws us today before Thine altar of spiritual understanding. May we vibrate to its divine attunement. We thank Thee for the privilege of having known the companionship of these now passed from mortal sight. Help us to sense in a very real way their presence in our midst today. To Thee be all honor, glory, and praise. Amen.

Reading:

Oft in the stilly night
  Ere slumber's chain has bound me,
Fond memory brings the light
  Of other days around me:
    The smiles, the tears,
    Of boyhood's years,
  The words of love then spoken;
    The eyes that shone,
    Now dimmed and gone,
  The cheerful hearts now broken.
Thus in the stilly night,
  Ere slumber's chain has bound me,
Sad memory brings the light
  Of other days around me.

When I remember all
  The friends so linked together
I've seen around me fall,
  Like leaves in wintry weather,
    I feel like one
    Who treads alone
  Some banquet-hall deserted,
    Whose lights are fled,
    Whose garlands dead,
  And all but he departed.
Thus in the stilly night,
  Ere slumber's chain has bound me,
Sad memory brings the light
  Of other days around me.

These beautiful words of the poet Moore, strike vividly into our hearts as we remember delightful days long gone from us.

Life here is like a wondrous kaleidoscope, reflecting the many forms and emotions of this experience. Mirrored in this reflection, and peopling its scenes, are those kindred spirits who grow into our hearts and lives. We have felt at home in their presence, and not as strangers in a strange land. As Whittier has put it,—those "who have made our home of life so pleasant."

It would be fearful indeed if we did not have a firm hope and faith in a future life, since passing and change are the inevitable destiny of mortal existence. We know that our friends, whose memories this occasion celebrates, are gone just a little beyond us on the pathway. We know that their love and memory of us still persist. We struggle on here seeking to learn the great lessons of spiritual truth, while they have gone to an immortal life of perfect health, of eternal youth, of everlasting advancement in wisdom, goodness, usefulness and happiness.

The memory of them stirs our hearts toward greater purpose and the contemplation of the joy that shall be ours when we shall gather with them over there in our spirit home. We cannot realize in its fullness the joy they know; an echo of it comes to us in the love we bear them. We feel within us a yearning to see them, to hear them speak to us, and to know again their presence beside us. All this is a part of the Divine message of Immortality, for this yearning spells the prophecy of a continued life. It speaks to our hearts the comforting assurance that "there is no death" to memory and love. There is "only a thin veil between us," and but for the vagueness of earth and flesh, we should know fully the truth that our loved ones walk at our side.

Someone has said "The only reality is consciousness." Yes, and in that reality our dear ones dwell as surely as we dwell in it at this moment. There is no death! Let us be persistent and earnest in proclaiming the wonderful truth. In its reality is the restoration of every cherished companion; indeed death does not divide the souls we love from ourselves.

There would be no honest sense or use in a memorial service to our loved ones, if the truth of immortality of the soul were not known and believed by us. Because we have received a sure word of recognition and remembrance from those gone on, we can joyfully meet today and name them in blessed remembrance.

Then for this reason we gratefully voice our love and tribute. We know that

" . . . ever near us though unseen,
   The dear immortal spirits tread,
For all the boundless universe
   Is life,—there are no dead."

Benediction:

In love and remembrance, bind our hearts closer together, O Infinite Love. May we so live that radiance and cheerfulness will shine upon all those we contact, making us worthy of those gone before, that we may some day hear their words of welcome saying, "Well done, faithful and true, enter thou into the joys prepared for thee in the Father's home of Light." Amen.

SERVICE OF ADMISSION
TO CHURCH MEMBERSHIP

NOTE: Upon invitation to candidates to come forward to the platform, the minister, or next proper officer of the church, may thus address them:

Friends, upon your pronounced faith in the principles of the religion of Spiritualism, and in the General Assembly of Spiritualists, its aims and its purposes, you are now being received into membership of this church.

We welcome the stand you have taken here to publicly testify to your sincerity in assuming certain obligations, such as every well-ordered spiritual organization imposes upon its members. You will be expected to live up to them steadfastly and honorably. You will find that no heavy tasks will be imposed upon you, for its yoke is easy and its burden light. To strive to love your fellowman and to be actively interested in forwarding the propagation of the truths of Spiritualism, become now your professed duties as members of this church. The essentials of the principles of religious living, in faith and application are particularly emphasized by us.

It is therefore in order that we ask you some questions, to which your public assent is required.

Questions:

1. Are you entirely satisfied in your own mind, through your experiences and understanding of the truth of spirit communication, that you wish it to become your avowed expression of religious faith?

2. Do you promise, insofar as it lies in your power, to conform to its teachings and practice?

3. Will you faithfully and cheerfully assist by contribution and personal effort, when called upon, to do all you can toward the furtherance of this church as an active body of the General Assembly of Spiritualists?

4. Do you affirm your acceptance of, and belief in its Declarations of Principles and Statements of Definition of Spiritualism, as enjoined by the General Assembly of Spiritualists?

5.   Do you promise to obey all the rules and regulations, as required by the Constitution and By-Laws of said organization and of this church?

NOTE: Having received due assent to these questions, the minister will address the candidates as follows:

Address to Candidate:

I now extend to you the right hand of fellowship and cordially welcome you into the membership of this church. May you always find here a spiritual and social welcome and that harmony which shall be conducive of spiritual progress and enlightenment. May the instructions in the truths of Spiritualism's Religion and Philosophy, which you find here, be of benefit and growth to you as you journey forward. Be not ashamed of Truth under whatever name it be sounded forth, nor withersoever it may lead you as an enlightened soul. Be faithful to duty, true to the trusts whose responsibility you now assume; show forth kindness and tolerance. Pray often and faint not. Strive to walk the path of sincerity in word and deed, seeking ever the riches of spiritual things and the vision of the realm of spiritual truth and happiness.

In the realization of God and Divine Truth you will find the means to overcome all obstacles in your path, and the healing and joy of your perfect spiritual being.

We bless you and rejoice with you that you have elected to stand and serve with us.

SPIRITUAL HEALING

Spiritualism's philosophy recognizes the fact of spiritual healing. It affirms that it is one of the psychic gifts which are the manifestation of mediumship. The early Christian church practiced this gift and Paul mentions it in his letter to the Corinthians, citing it among the "spiritual gifts" to be looked for as the manifestation of the power of God and evidenced in the Christian church. 1st Corinthians, 12.

    4. Now there are diversities of gifts, but the same Spirit.

    9. To another faith by the same Spirit, to another the gifts of *healing* by the same Spirit."

This gift is exercised through the instrumentality of the medium whose peculiar powers are manifested in magnetic vibration. Augmented with these powers are forces of spirit, such as the personal influence of excarnate spiritual beings, for the relief and cure of mental and physical diseases.

The "laying on of hands" was practised by the leaders of the Christian religion, and thereby, so they taught and believed, spiritual power was brought into direct contact with mortal bodies.

To forbid the exercise of spiritual healing as a spiritual gift, is to restrict the rights of the religionist who believes and practices his faith, both as a Christian and a Spiritualist.

Healing Affirmation:

"Health, Happiness, and Peace, are the Divine heritage of the Father.

Vibrating through me is the immortal current of Everlasting Life and the fullness of Spiritual Perfection."

"I am one with the Infinite."

"I ask the Great Divine Healing Force to calm all disturbing fears, to tranquilize thoughts and nerves, Creating unobstructed pathways of spiritual vibration, and to restore me to perfect health.

I ask this in all sincerity, and faithfully I will do my part."

"I ask the Great Divine Healing Force to help all those in need of spiritual strength and bodily perfection, whether absent or present at this hour, and to restore them to perfect health."

There is no question as to the great benefits that have and are being accomplished by Spiritual Healing. The power of prayer is unlimited. It is recommended that Healing shall be done by prayer and not through the laying on of hands.

HOW SHALL WE TEACH SPIRITUALISM?

By REV. CONVERSE E. NICKERSON

"The spirit's ladder
That from this gross and physical world of dust
Even to the starry world, with thousand rounds
Builds itself up; on which the unseen powers
Move up and down on heavenly ministeries—
The circles in the circles, that approach
The central sun from ever narrowing orbits."

—Coleridge

A correct knowledge of the philosophy of Spiritualism could add greatly to the happiness of all mankind. The understanding of the religion of Spiritualism could bring peace and a complete confidence in God.

The "spirit's ladder builds itself," the poet tells us; its sure influence colors all philosophy and all true poetry of the soul. The unseen powers that move up and down its rounds are on errands of heavenly ministry. Woven into the philosophy evolved by man here on earth, are the great tales of the soul's eternal pilgrimage. Circles within circles are the various advanced stages of the soul's development and progress. From his physical world of dust, on upward to the starry world, the message of immortality rings its sweet notes echoing the happiness awaiting the anxious mortals of earth. Mortals, did I say? No, not mortals, but living, earnest spirits encased in mortality, who wait for the summons that shall declare that "death's pale reign is o'er and joy unutterable is the portion of God's offspring!"

How shall we teach this great truth so that all who hear us will be converted by its message? Surely not alone by the physical demonstration, since many who receive it in that way must confess to the doubtings that of necessity come.

The pure message of communication, bearing with it indisputable truth, both of identity and purport, is the only message that Spiritualism should claim. The prevalence of the fraudulent has frightened away from us many who would become sincere Spiritualists.

Ten or twelve personal messages are sufficient at any public Spiritualist service. These, if convincing, can amply repay everyone who attends such a service, witnessing such genuine spirit communication. We make a mistake by allowing our mediums to promise in their advertising that "everyone present will receive a message." Long and dull Spiritualist meetings do not help the cause.

The attitude of the sincere Spiritualist will be one of worship; a desire to study spiritual truth.

Sometimes we have been told that we need to get more of the *right* people to believe in Spiritualism. Well, who are the *right* people? Wherever we find anyone desiring to learn spiritual truth, there is a *right* person. But we must put forward the *right* sort of presentation in order to attract this *right* kind of person. If there is a difficulty within our ranks to build and support solid Spiritualist churches and the needful branches of a successful religious movement, then it should be the deep concern of every true Spiritualist to remedy this situation.

The message-hunting element must give place to the church member. The uneducated would-be leader must give place to a trained and intellectually awakened minister who will serve the cause of Spiritualism just as efficiently as a minister of some other denomination.

We must emphasize the fact that Spiritualism is a religion and that its great office in the world is to be the means by which its adherents worship God. If we boast of a church and call ourselves a denomination that believes in God,—Infinite Intelligence,—then we are duty-bound to establish churches and conduct them as such.

We must recognize some central doctrine or religious book. It is vain to cry "religion" and at the same time refuse the spiritual principles of religion. The New Testament is as much the book of the Spiritualist as it is of any other believer in God. If we scorn the teachings of righteousness as taught by Jesus Christ, how shall we attract Christian living people who are round about us? They are asking if Spiritualists have any religion. In derision they have named us "spiritists." Our respectful title is Spiritualists,—with a capital S, for we are a denomination of worshippers.

The Mormons have their text-book which is the "Book of Mormon." The Christian Scientists have their text-book which is "Science and Health." The Spiritualists must center around some definite book of philosophy also. Here in this Manual of The General Assembly of Spiritualists we have gathered the foundational principles of our religion. Everyone who chooses may attach himself to those principles and form a solid body of worshippers toward the end that Spiritualism may grow as a denomination of consistent worshippers of God.

The Spiritualist must know for himself what he believes, what principles of truth found in his declaration of faith are fully accepted by him. In that way only can he be progressive as a Spiritualist. He must be willing to renounce any former church denomination when he becomes a Spiritualist. A Spiritualist cannot be undecided in this matter, unless he is using Spiritualism for merely something to satisfy his curiosity.

A true Spiritualist can embrace a form of baptism. If we christen our babies, why not a ceremony for our conversion to Spiritualism? Baptism has been the religious rite of those who become Christians. We can also institute some form of it as an initiation ceremony into the Spiritualist church.

We do accept most of the other Christian observances which have centered around Christ and his disciples and that first church which kept alive the faith of a future life.

The opposite to spiritual things is materialism. We are either a believer in the reality of the spiritual or we are materialists. Then, believing in spiritual realities we worship in a spiritual manner.

All truth discerned by man comes to him upon the framework of science and so, when we say Spiritualism is a science, that is what we have said, and all that can be implied. But the truth itself, if it appeals to the soul, must partake of philosophy. If it satisfies the soul it is *religion*. Therefore the Religion of Spiritualism is its greatest asset. We may color the truths of that religion with the teachings of Confucius, or Plato, or Jesus, but wherever truth is found, we can as God's children, justly lay claim to it.

The truth in the "23rd Psalm" or the "Sermon on the Mount" will bring food to the Spiritualist as well as it does to the Methodist. The beauty of any and all truth found in Scripture is needful for the soul of the Spiritualist, why make unnecessary admission?

We have spirit communication that other denominations which believe in Christ, have not. With it we will hold to righteous living and the practice of the spiritual laws of the soul, even as Jesus taught them.

JESUS OF NAZARETH

By REV. CONVERSE E. NICKERSON

We believe and teach that the establishment of the Christian Church was brought about by a great outpouring of spirit power; also that the leader of this marvelous season of spirit manifestation was the psychic Jesus. His promise to his followers of "Greater things than I do, shall ye also do," meant in a very definite way that the so-called miracles which he and his disciples wrought were of the express power and at the dictation of the spirit world.

That such a person as Jesus once lived and taught, there can be little doubt. Secular history has recorded his name and such witnesses as Josephus, Tacitus, and Polycarp, demand serious consideration.

Publius Tacitus, Roman historian who lived about the last part of the first century, makes direct reference to Jesus. He states:

"The Christians of Nero's day traced their origin to one named Christ, who was put to death by Pontius Pilate during the reign of Tiberius Caesar."

The Encyclopedia Britannica affirms that "Tacitus is to be trusted in his statement of facts."

Josephus, Jewish historian, lived earlier than Tacitus, and was born in Jerusalem in 37 A.D. Josephus bears this testimony of Mary's son:

"At this time lived Jesus, a wise man, if indeed it is proper to call him a man: for he was a doer of wonderful works and a teacher of men who received the truth gladly. He won to himself both many Jews and many Greeks. This was the Christ. And when Pilate, on⁻ the indictment of the chief man among us, sentenced him to crucifixion, those who love him, at first, did not cease loving him, for he appeared to them alive again the third day, as indeed the prophets had foretold,—these and other wonders concerning him. Even unto this day the race of Christians named for him are not extinct."

Josephus knew what had been going on during his century; the influence of Jesus' trial and death, and the stir it caused in Jerusalem, was still a matter of great moment in the minds of the people. The Jews were not able to forget the shadow of the cross and factions and sects were still affected by the teachings of the Man of Nazareth.

Jesus was the oldest of four brothers, whose names were James, Joses, Judas, and Simeon. (See Matthew 13:55. He also had two sisters, (see verse 56 of same chapter.)

He was called "the carpenter's son" and recognized during his lifetime as the "son of Joseph and Mary." In the first chapter of the gospel of Matthew we find a genealogy sketching the "line of David the Jewish king" down to "Joseph, the husband of Mary",—parents of Jesus. Since Joseph is not recognized as the parental father of Jesus, how then can any lineage be established between Jesus and King David?

In the book of Acts we read: "The former treatise have I made, O Theophilus, of all that Jesus began to do and teach."—Acts 1:1.

Of all the New Testament writers whose writings could least have been tampered with, Paul stands alone. This apostle of Jesus steadfastly wrote and preached about the personal Jesus. He tells vividly of his persecution of Jesus and the disciples of the Master. Paul dramatically testified before Agrippa that Jesus called to him from the spirit world: Read Acts 26, 1st to 22nd verse.

We never need doubt that Shakespeare wrote the plays attributed to his authorship. Shall we not then feel the same certainty about most of the glorious truths of spiritual God-apportioned wisdom which was voiced through this great inspirational psychic of Nazareth?

Spiritualism's proof does not rest alone upon the advent, and life, and return from spirit, of Jesus. Nor does such proof depend solely upon the fact that the whole Bible is full of the experiences of motals who conversed with the so-called dead, and with angels from higher spheres of life-consciousness. These great truths have been known by all nations and by all ages of mankind, as Samuel Johnson, the English philosopher, pointed out. We are poor students of philosophical truth if we rudely and wilfully trample upon the beautiful personality of Jesus Christ, simply because we have become prejudiced against the Bible and the creeds of the Christian Church.

Jesus is called the Christ because of his divine teachings. He swept through the lives and experiences of those who heard him speak, as no man of his time, or since his day. His teachings are still thrilling the world of thought. Some standard of righteousness must serve as the beacon toward which the souls of men are attracted. That standard Jesus established; its logic and spiritual force has never been equaled nor doubted.

One does not need to believe in the virgin birth of Jesus in order to understand and be blessed by his glorious utterances. If, through something he taught, I can find the true use and help of prayer for my soul, I shall be bountifully aided onward in my daily progression toward that day when I lay this physical body by and enter the fuller expression of spirit.

For the success of Spiritualism as a religion, its adherents must build upon the facts of its great argument for the survival of the personality after the change called death. There must be a steadfast affirmation of Spiritualism as a religion, also, if mankind is to worship God at its shrine. Spiritualists must love it and work for it as zealously as other religionists work for theirs; they must seek to carry our gospel to the minds of thinking people and develop a respect and regard for the truths of Spiritualism before the world.

Jesus establishes spiritual truth before the world. In addition to this, his death and return from his Father's Kingdom unequivocally pronounce the truth of the Spiritualist's gospel,—the so-called dead live!

Sublime spiritual manifestation marked his baptism of John in the Jordan River, consecrating him as prophet and divine example; it dedicated his life to the service of the great celestial hosts of heaven. Through him as an instrument were to flow the precepts and preachings of spiritual wisdom and power.

Complete in psychic development he was the great demonstration of what the bridge of communication means. The great test was made on the Mount of Transfiguration when he led his three chosen friends, Peter and John and James, into the sweet mysteries of spirit communion.

"And the fashion of his countenance was altered, and his raiment was white and glistening." Here was spirit power made visible to mortal sight!

There in their midst appeared "two men which were Moses and Elias." This is evidence beyond dispute. Its testimony bears witness through Jesus that spirit communication is certain.

Then, finally, we hear Him plead in agony of physical death, "My God, why has Thou forsaken me." We know then that mortally he died. We know that even in this tragic moment he is still the example of the change called death, the only means whereby he can fulfill his enlightened promise that souls are immortal. This is the last great act of the material scene. When next he appears, he must come as the risen spirit. This culminates his sacred mission.

No recorded witness in the Gospel story could testify that he saw the crucified body of Jesus rise from the tomb, open its eyes, speak, and proclaim itself conqueror of death. His recorded appearances are all of spirit,—the celestial comforter returning to prove the inheritance of immortality!

Without the spirit return of Jesus and the proved identification of his personality there would have been no survival of his teachings and the Christian Church. Therefore the Christian Church rests its testimony of truth upon the proclamation of spirit return and personal survival.

Invocation:

O Infinite Spirit of Wisdom, whom we call Father, God, bless us this day as we wait on Thee. Attune our hearts to that high atmosphere of Eternal Love, that we too may share in the shedding abroad of its fullness and power; that on its wings may come a healing and a peace. Open our spiritual vision that we may see the radiance of Thy glory in all things. Grant to us the great comfort and joy of the consciousness of angel helpers. Allow us to know for ourselves that our dear and loved ones are near us, closely making their companionship of love and assurance the benediction of this earthly pilgrimage. Come into our midst, O spiritual powers, and heal all our diseases; dry all our tears, and harmonize our doubts and shortcomings into complete knowledge and understanding. We thank Thee for spiritual Truth, and that we have been led in the paths of its holy light. In the name of the Christ Spirit, O God, and the Angel World. Amen.

Our Heavenly Father, Creator, and Souls' Light, lift us up this day, we pray Thee, to the heights of spiritual understanding. May our hearts be renewed within us and a song of joy and thanksgiving be upon our lips. May the living moments of this Present teach us Wisdom and Love. Upon the Wings of the Morning may we be lifted up. O may we join our songs with the singing of the angels of Thine eternal Heaven. Let the harmonious beams of spiritual light and understanding draw us closer together as neighbor and friend. May that oneness of spirit and the singleness of spiritual endeavor be ours for the furtherance of Thy Kingdom on earth. We ask it in Thy name, Our Father. Amen.

THE 23rd PSALM

The Lord is my shepherd; I shall not want.

He maketh me to lie down in green pastures; he leadeth me beside the still waters.

He restoreth my soul; he leadeth me in the paths o righteousness for His name's sake.

Yes, though I walk through the valley of the shadow of death, I will fear no evil: for Thou art with me;

Thy rod and Thy staff they comfort me.

Thou preparest a table before me in the presence of mine enemies: thou anointest my head with oil; my cup runneth over.

Surely goodness and mercy shall follow me all the days of my life: and I will dwell in the house of the Lord forever.

This is the Psalm of confidence and spiritual power. It warms the heart and brings a definite brightness of thought, as we contemplate the spiritual content of these beautiful words.

The Lord (God) is my shepherd, and since I rest completely in Him, through Him I have my life and being, I shall not want. All things that are necessary for the happiness of my soul are ready at hand for my partaking.

The sweetness of "green pastures" can bless me with their refreshing strength, whenever I turn to them. They are the comforting pastures of Divine confidence and safety. True to His own assurance, God, my Heavenly Father, "leadeth me in the paths of righteousness." His name is Spirit, and He surrounds my soul with spiritual understanding. This understanding refreshes me and builds within me all power and illumination.

To my soul, Death is an unreality, and only its shadow can come near me. I shall "walk through its valley" and fear no evil. God is forever with me, sustaining and blessing me with the outpouring of His Love and strength.

Jesus instructed me to call Him my Heavenly Father.

"His rod and His staff" constantly guard and guide me. I find in Him correction and support in every condition of this life. His will makes itself known to me in the channels of impression and discernment.

"In the presence of mine enemies," I have a table of blessing and good things that the enemies of Peace and Righteousness see not. When the storms are heavy and the wild winds of material adversity rush around me, there is that inner strength and consolation that is as a table of spiritual sustenance.

The oil of gladness is poured upon me in overflowing measure; a little meditation and I realize with grateful thanks how good my Heavenly Father is — "my cup runneth over."

I know that onward, as long as I shall live upon the earth, there is the never-failing arm of God to sustain me. "Goodness and mercy shall follow me," in their radiance I shall find progression and truth. I shall never lack, and therefore I need never be discouraged.

My soul is immortal, for He hath declared it, — "I will dwell in the house of the Lord (God) forever!" There is a place prepared for me and I am destined to dwell in it.

God's love hath declared this and His Spirit hath designed the revealment of it to the sons of men. In the heavenly mansions of the Father's house of Light, where glory and power, and love and happiness dwell, is my eternal home and habitation.

Rev. Converse E. Nickerson

Offertory Blessings:

With these our gifts we consecrate
Our hearts to Thee, our Father dear;
May this our offering dedicate
In love our service here.
To Thee, O God, our prayers shall rise,
Our thankfulness be known;
Whatever bountiful be ours
We but give back Thine own. Amen.

May these gifts be a symbol of our earnestness toward Thee, Our
Father. Let their use, in Thy holy name, carry forth a spiritual blessing.
In love and gratitude to Thee and the angel world for unnumbered
blessings, we give thee thanks. Amen.

Benedictions:

To Him who is able to keep us and guard us, may we render all
thanks and adoration; and to the angel world, whose love surrounds
us, we commend our paths.

May the light of God's love and the purity of His grace, rest
upon us as we depart from this service. Guard our minds and hearts
with spiritual desires and charitable conduct. This we ask in the name
of all Goodness and Truth. Amen.

May the peace that passeth all understanding bless us and watch
over us as we go from here; under the wings of eternal Love, may we
find health and contentment. This we ask in the name of the Spirit
of Christ. Amen.

May the glorious presence of angel friends, the communion of
exalted souls, and the comfort of God's Holy Spirit, abide with us,
cleansing our hearts from all fear, and drawing us nearer to the realization of the Divine. May Peace, Mercy, and Everlasting Love watch
over us. Amen.

MARRIAGE SERVICE NUMBER ONE

NOTE: Only ordained ministers may perform the marriage ceremony. All ministers qualified in accordance with the laws of the General Assembly of Spiritualists to perform the marriage service should inform themselves regarding state and municipal laws, where they are called upon to officiate and comply therewith, in order to assure the legality of the marriage.

NOTE: Ordination into the ministry of the Gospel of Spiritualism is specifically obtained through and by the Board of the General Assembly of Spiritualists.

Marriage Ceremony

The Minister shall say:

Beloved Friends, we have met here this day in the sight of God and the Angel World, to join together this man and this woman in holy matrimony. Matrimony is an esteemed and honorable estate to all those who enter it reverently, discreetly, and soberly. With a true faith in God and in this holy estate, these two persons present come now to be joined. If any one can show just cause why they may not lawfully be joined together let him now speak, or else hereafter forever hold his peace. (Pause.)

The Minister shall then say to the couple before him:

I require and charge you both most solemnly, that if either of you know of any just reason why you may not lawfully be joined together in matrimony, that you now confess it. For, be most certainly assured, that if any persons are joined together otherwise than spiritually and morally, rightfully in God's sight, their marriage is not lawful.

The Minister, addressing the man by his Christian name, shall say to him:

------------------------, wilt thou have this woman to be thy wedded wife, promising faithfully to cherish and to comfort and to protect her in sickness and in health; and forsaking all others, keep thee only unto her, as long as you both shall live?

Answer: "I will."

The Minister, addressing the woman by her Christian name, shall say unto her:

----------------------, wilt thou have this man to be thy wedded husband, promising faithfully to cherish and to comfort and to minister unto him in sickness and in health; forsaking all others, keep thee only unto him, as long as you both shall live?

Answer: I will.

The Minister shall then say:

Who giveth this woman to be married to this man?

The father or a friend of the woman shall say:

I do.

The Minister, joining the woman's right hand with the right hand of the man, shall say: (the man repeating in response.)

I, ----------------------, take thee, ----------------------, to be my wedded wife, to have and to hold from this day forth, for better for worse, for richer for poorer, in sickness and in health, to love and cherish, till death do us part; and thereto I plight thee my troth.

Then shall they loose hands and the woman, with her right hand taking the man by his right hand, shall likewise repeat in response to the Minister's word:

I, ----------------------, take thee, ----------------------, to be my wedded husband, to have and to hold from this day forth, for better for worse, for richer for poorer, in sickness and in health, to love and cherish, till death do us part; and thereto I plight my troth.

Then shall the man place upon the fourth finger of the woman's left hand a ring, and holding it there, repeat in response to the Minister's words:

With this ring, I thee wed, in the name of Our Heavenly Father and the Angel World.

The Minister shall say:

Whom God hath joined together, let no man put asunder. Forasmuch as----------------------and----------------------have consented together to be joined in the bonds of holy wedlock, and thereto have pledged their troth, each to the other, I pronounce that they are husband and wife, in the witness and blessing of God and the Angel World. Amen.

The Minister may add his blessing with the following benediction:

Blessed angel witnesses, here we invoke thy benediction and solicitous care over these who have now entered into that spiritual and joyous estate of marriage, to walk together the path of this earthly pilgrimage. Be with them in loving counsel when they shall seek thine aid. Comfort and bless them whenever possible with thy cheerful thoughts, that they may be encouraged to walk onward in the sunshine of the knowledge that Life is to be lived in co-operation and helpfulness, sharing one another's burdens and sorrows. Bring unto them a new song of joy in the fellowship and spiritual communion of two souls blessed by mutual love and endeavor. Amen.

Wedding Song

I saw two clouds at morning
Tinged with the rising sun;
And in the dawn they floated on
And mingled into one;
I thought that morning cloud was blest,
It moved so sweetly to the west.

I saw two summer currents
Flow smoothly to their meeting,
And join their course with silent force,
In peace each other greeting;
Calm was their course through banks of green
While dimpling eddies played between.

Such be your gentle motion,
Till life's last pulse shall beat;
Like summer's beam and summer's stream
Float on, in joy, to meet
A calmer sea, where storms shall cease;
A purer sky, where all is peace!

—Brainard

MARRIAGE SERVICE NUMBER TWO

(See Instructions at beginning of Services)

Minister:

My friends, you have been asked to witness the ceremony of marriage between William_____ and Elizabeth_____. Having made their choice of a life mate they have now come before us in public acknowledgment of their intentions toward matrimony. In this holy estate we now witness this ceremony. If any there be who can show just cause why these two should not be joined together in marriage, let him speak forth, or else hold his peace. (Pause.)

Minister to the man:

Marriage, blessed and sanctioned by spiritual law and recognized as the security bond of society, is an honorable estate. Jesus Christ was glad to be present at such a ceremony, making known thereby that it is good for two souls to be joined in hallowed love and companionship. The perfection of life here on earth demands all that the estate of marriage may honorably bring forth. In domestic loyalty and affection is anchored felicity and happiness.

Such a step must not lightly be entered into; but with the calm and measured judgment, born of the flame of true love, shall those so minded step forth into the responsibilities and the joys of wedded partnership. Forbearance, patience, and a mutual esteem, are some of the foundation principles on which is builded a firm and enduring happiness of marriage.

May your wedded life be bound with the silken cords of affection, and the firm ties of confidence and love. So will the sunlight of your middle years be radiant with spiritual strength, refreshing, sustaining, and brightening that eventide of life for you, when, together, hand in hand, you bravely walk toward the sunset.

To this young man, let me say: Love and cherish her whom God has privileged you to claim as your bride this day. Make her the adoring shrine of that home and household which hereby you shall lay the foundation stone. Your domestic bliss alone can be made secure by your fidelity and love. To this you must dedicate your years of wedded association.

To this young woman, let me say, love him, cherish him,—a loving heart, is a woman's greatest wedded treasure. Guard it well with that sincerity of mind and intent which will make true appreciation and love ever uppermost. Love, if nurtured alone, lives fleetingly; joined with that reciprocal affection which makes a man cleave unto a woman, and she to him, that they may be closely bound in the soul-ties of abiding love. It is a living essence of eternal and spiritual truth.

To you both, let me say, May you prove to your great soul satisfaction how bountiful true love is. A life well lived is the crowning glory of this earthly expression; marriage well lived is the double expression of that glory. We, your friends, wish you every happiness; that the evening of life may find you, surrounded in the affection of children and friends, warm in the healing balm of a lifetime of love.

Now, I charge you, as you both shall answer to your conscience in the after life, that if you two know of any reason why you may not lawfully be joined together in matrimony, you confess it now. (Pause.)

Minister to the man:

Do you, William_____ take this woman whom you now hold by the hand, to be your wife and companion, the partner of your joys and sorrows, and shall it be your constant desire to cherish her, holding yourself only for her, from this time forth? (Man answers, I do.)

Do you pledge yourself ever to honor, love, and protect her in sickness and in health, in prosperity and in adversity, henceforth, so long as you both shall live? (Man answers, I do.)

Minister to the woman:

Do you, Elizabeth_____ take this man whom you now hold by the hand, to be your husband and companion, the partner of your joys and sorrows, and shall it be your constant desire to cherish and care for him, holding yourself only for him, from this time forth? (Woman answers, I do.)

Do you pledge yourself ever to honor, love and minister unto him in sickness and in health, in prosperity and in adversity, henceforth, as long as you both shall live? (Woman answers, I do.)

(Minister requests the wedding ring, then gives it to the man with the direction to place it on the fourth finger of his bride's left hand.)

Minister continues:

Inasmuch as you have pledged between you this marriage troth, and have given and received a ring in token of the same, I, by the authority vested in me as a Minister of the Gospel of Spiritualism, and in accordance with the laws of this state, do now pronounce you, William_____ and Elizabeth_____ to be Husband and Wife.

May the blessings of our Angel Messengers of Peace and Spiritual Direction be with you both from this day forth.

May joy and bountiful happiness be yours, increasing your material and spiritual possessions. Amen.

Bridal Benediction

O hallowed by thy wedded life
That now is joined in "man and wife,"
That now is made a joyful "one,"
To last till life on earth is done;
For while you journey side by side,
As dear to each may you abide.
The rose its sweetness draws from sun,
So shall your joy from love be spun;
Not singly but together be
Knit soul to soul, contentedly;
Love's benediction o'er you spread,
Thus perfect marriage, truly wed.
Come joy or sorrow, ever pray
Neither from other e'er will stray;
Sharing each comfort, sharing each fear,
Lending of courage, hope and cheer;
Peace, joy, and happiness all the way,
Is my wish to you this Wedding Day!

Rev. Converse E. Nickerson

CHRISTENING SERVICE

How sweet in the morning time of life it is to see these bright jewels of innocence. They are like the sparkling gems that reflect the beauty of some fairy-land where eternal youth reigns supreme. Children are the bright shafts of sunshine that sweeten the spiritual atmospheres of our earth life. These gentle blossoms adorn and make pleasant the beautiful regions through which we pass on our earth pilgrimage!

At this present hour we invoke the spiritual presence of those pure and wise spirits of light that they may guide us in inspiration as we bestow upon this little one the dedication and blessing symbolized by this service of christening and baptism.

May this young and innocent life, so newly beginning the earth expression, be guarded and sustained by thee, O blessed angels! Bring forward thy strengthening and protective band of bright celestial souls that they may bless and assist this little bud to flower forth in beauty and spiritual power; may there be unfolded to its gradual understanding the impressive mysteries of life, in its journeyings onward and upward.

Minister's address to the Parents:

We address you, the parents (or guardian) of this child, and earnestly, yea solemnly, remind you that in your care and trust must rest the responsibility of the spiritual upbringing of this little one. On you must fall the duty of placing before the child mind those spiritual truths of life that shall evermore be the staff of strength and understanding; you will be instrumental in helping to fashion the path of its soul destiny.

As this little one came into this world welcomed and blessed by the smiles and prayers of those expectant and anxious to receive it, so may it continue to have that light of love and solicitation shine round about it as long as it shall stay among you.

Children are a divine heritage. They are the loving token of our Heavenly Father's love. His wisdom hath prepared all things; it sent you forth that you might prepare the way, even as others preceded you; so is lengthened and suspended the chain of life, which is the expression of God.

That the will of God be done on earth as it is in Heaven, shall ye strive faithfully to surround this dear one with thoughts and with deeds productive of spiritual things. Bless it with your knowledge and experience, and the fruits of your spiritual intuition.

Now we consecrate the life of this little one to purity and to truth. Only through those avenues of understanding can he (or she) be brought into happiness and a useful service to others.

Minister shall take the bowl of flowers (or water if preferred) and dropping the petals over the child, shall say:

Here in the presence of these witnesses, both heavenly and earthly, I christen you (giving the name of the child) and dedicate you to the service of spiritual things. Herewith may you receive the blessing of the angel world.

In beauty, in love, in tender regard, receive you our blessing.

> Radiant angels, ever near,
> Come to guard, to bless and cheer;
> Hold in love thy gracious care
> O'er this darling, sweet and fair.
> Open wide the heavenly strand;
> Pour its favors, rich and grand,
> Here like dew refreshing sweet, —
> Love's bright path for little feet.

Jesus Christ, the master of spiritual teaching, said,

"Suffer little children, and forbid them not, to come unto me: for of such is the kingdom of heaven." And he placed his hands upon their heads and blessed them.

And so, in the knowledge, fellowship, and steadfastness of our spiritual truth, and the holy guidance of risen friends, the angel host, we go forth from this service.

Amen.

FUNERAL SERVICE

NOTE: Arrange for hymns and instrumental music as desired.

Address:

Friends, we gather to pay our respectful tribute of love and meditation, in memory of our dear brother (or sister).

We would not center our thoughts upon the dark and dismal side in considering that event of change that has come to one who moved so brightly and so lovingly among us. We would rather bear in remembrance the beauty and the safety of the great things of God, — His laws and His blessings, — as we talk of this change called death.

The Psalmist has written:

"Yea though I walk through the valley and the shadow of death, I will fear no evil, for Thou art with me."

The soul is secure in the great ocean of the Love of God the Father. Socrates declared that "no evil can happen to a good man, either in his life, or after his death." The poet sings, "No harm can come to me on ocean or on shore." Jesus taught his diciples the comforting truth, "Let not your hearts be troubled, ye believe in God."

The great central truth of life is the living presence of conscious spirit. That living presence we have been acquainted with. Now, in the pallor of physical death, we seek for it in vain. It has fled away into another room of God's great house. Invisible to mortal senses, it still beams its radiance, and still is conscious of living and of habitation under the eternal laws of the Creator.

Immortality must intimately concern the soul of man. To live in God and in Him have our being means that through His laws we find our expression of existence. So then, for our brother we know today that he lives.

A glorious adventure has been entered into. Onward, through the valley and the shadow of death, this dear one has wended his way. Into the brightness of the glory of the eternal things of God, he has found that larger life which awaits all of us.

We should rejoice that immortality is our inheritance from the hand of God. We are His children, and for us He has created the great law of love and life. To love is the token of the enduring existence of immortality. Loving, we express God, and through love we communicate our spiritual presence in its true reality. Because we love one another, the heart is touched with grief at separation; our tears are those begotten of love, but our hopes are those of the eternal blessings, even yet to be bestowed upon us through the continued association and companionship of those we love.

We come in confidence today, therefore, knowing that "to be absent from the body is to be present" in spirit with those gone on before. Truly arisen, are they, and they do await the full consummation of their joy when we shall go to them and thus all be reunited forever in the spiritual kingdom of the Father.

"And I John, saw a new heaven and a new earth: for the first heaven and the first earth were passed away."

This is the first earth, upon which we tread. There shall be a new earth, — a new expression of existence. Our earthly garments shall be changed for those of immortal vesture.

"And God shall wipe away all tears from their eyes; and there shall be no more death, neither sorrow nor crying, neither shall there be any more pain: for the former things have passed away."

"And the angel said, Write, for these things are true and faithful."

The religion of Spiritualism teaches exactly this truth: death is abolished in the understanding of the true laws of life. This cold form of clay has no recognition, nor spiritual life in it. It is the garment once used by the departed. It enfolds him no more. He has stepped away to a higher expression of his being. In that expression of life he will weep no more. His tears of sorrow are dissolved in the spiritual truth and confidence of his true spiritual existence. He now knows that the former things are passed away.

But love and joyful remembrance, recognition, aspiration, and wisdom, are his in far greater measure than they could have been while limited by the bonds of earth.

And so we do not say "he is dead." He is just away.

It is ours to reflect with knowledge and assurance upon this true meaning of life. Full confidence, and not despair, is read from these indications of God's love and eternal care for us.

"Surely goodness and mercy shall follow me all the days of my life: and I will dwell in the house of God forever."

Invocation:

O eternal Father, bear us up on the wings of love today. Let us see through our tears the rainbow of Thy love and protection, that in the midst of the mystery of Death we will take courage. Comfort us with the consciousness of the presence of loved ones in spirit; may we know they stand closely about us, smiling their love into our hearts. Scatter the darkness and reveal the light of Thy countenance, as we wait before Thee. When the lonely hours come in which the physical form of our loved one is missed, may we be strengthened by the knowledge that he is not dead, — only gone a little way before us on the journey. We ask for peace, spiritual progression, understanding, and love, in this hour.

Thine be the glory, the praise and the spiritual homage. Amen.

COMMITTAL SERVICE

"There is a natural body and there is a spiritual body. How be it, that which was first was not spiritual, but the natural, and afterward the spiritual." So we reverently commit to earth the natural body. In loving memory of our risen brother we mark this mortal resting place, while we look upward in confidence and understanding toward the spiritual heights of his eternal habitation.   Amen.

"O Love that wilt not let me go,
  I rest my weary soul in Thee,
  I give Thee back the life I owe
  That in thine ocean depths its flow
  May richer, fuller be."

Benediction:

May spiritual counsellors go with you to your homes, dispelling the sorrows and the shadows from your hearts. May you find peace and joy in spiritual communion, thus drawing nearer to that realm into which our beloved has entered. May eternal Joy illumine your pathway, mantling you with that peace that passeth all understanding, now and ever more.   Amen.

For One Well Known

We seem to give *him* back to thee, dear God, who gavest *him* to us. Yet as thou didst not lose *him* in giving, so we have not lost *him* by *his* return. For what is thine is ours always; and life is eternal and love is immortal; and what we sometimes call death is only a horizon, and a horizon is nothing but the limit of our sight. Lift us up, O God, that we may see further; cleanse our eyes that we may see more clearly; draw us closer to thyself that we may know ourselves nearer to our beloved who are with thee, that where they are, and thou art, we too may be.

FUNERAL SERVICE FOR A CHILD

NOTE: Arrange for hymns and instrumental music as desired.

Bible Reading:

"Then there were brought unto him little children, that he should put his hands on them and pray; and the disciples rebuked them.
"But Jesus said, Suffer little children, and forbid them not, to come unto me: for of such is the kingdom of heaven." Matthew 19:13, 14.

"For of such is the kingdom of heaven." How beautiful are these words as applied to children! The freshness of beautiful flowers is in the beauty and youth of children. Theirs is the eternal picture of life as we would always want to keep it; a life free from the withering hand of age and decay; gentle as the morning breeze; bright as the early beams of the morning sun; laughing and gay as the song of the birds; — all this, and more, is revealed in the lives of little children.

The weighty questionings of adult life, and all its responsibilities, are unknown to childhood. Worry and care do not press down the gentle brows of these smiling little ones. Life has not laid its heavy hand upon the heart of a little child.

To be withdrawn from the more serious scenes of mortal existence is to be preserved from the cares and concerns that make weary this earthly pilgrimage.

Jesus, the loving teacher of spiritual truth, knew this. He recognized the simple purity and blessedness of children. Their stainless souls were unsullied by the storm and temptations that afflict those who are granted longer experiences in this vale of tears.

It is hard for those who mourn the seperation which comes when these tender blossoms depart from the garden of earthly life; there is an aching void which seems never to be filled. Often years must pass, with all the wiser lessons learned, before it is possible to understand how kindly God's love and protection has been manifested.

These tender flowers are but transplanted to that more lovely Eden of God, there to grow into the fullness of beauty.

We know that all things are safe with God. His laws and His providence are all inclusive. His eternal name is LOVE; and the sweetness of His love has appeared unto us in the form of children in this plan of His creation. Because God loves, we must trust Him to safely take care of these sweet flowers of His kingdom,—"for of such is the kingdom of heaven."

Since we know that little children and babes must die, death then, must be gentle with them. It cannot be the harsh blight and destroyer our first fears would picture it to be. With kindly caress these little ones are carried over into the happy land of spirit. Bright angels walk beside them, holding them close. The wonder and the beauty of that glorious home soothes away fear and distrust. Sweet music echoes back the happiness of their little hearts and they "sing a new and happy song."

We would remember through our tears, familiar voices, words oft repeated, and smiling faces. These shall be surely restored to us, for in reality they have never perished, — only faded from our mortal vision.

In that sunrise morning when we too shall continue our pilgrimage into the realms of celestial light, these precious ones will be there to greet us, and their glad voices will join that welcome which echoes the everlasting praise of our loving Heavenly Father.

The wisdom of God gave us the family circle, and His great Divine Mind of Love will continue it beyond the ravages of Time and Mortality.

May we be inspired by the love of this young life. May that inspiration unseal the fountain of love in our hearts so that we walk more cheerfully and lovingly with one another. Let our word of kindness help to heal the spirits of those who walk beside us, making truer the vision of our journey.

Our darling will then not have lived in vain, but the sweet incense of its little life shall nurture the spiritual brightness of those who have loved it so dearly.

In the quiet musings of eventide, when rest is near, you will hear the whispering of sweet childish voices chanting for you a song of comfort. The peace that passeth all understanding will be yours for the message of that Song will make you to know that there is no death.

Invocation:

O Infinite Spirit of Eternal Love, breathe upon us today. Take away sorrow from our hearts, and wipe away the mourner's tear. Raise our vision to the heavenly heights that we may glimpse the beauty of that land where our little one now dwells. Let us realize something of the truth of the greater mission in store for our dear one. The perfect day which banishes all night has come and in it, safely abiding, is the smiling face of this blossom. There is no night there, and so we too would look toward the true spiritual day; may its brightness shine in our hearts, making pure the emotions within us. Hallow the place left vacant by the passing on of this little one, that peace may grow with us. We thank Thee, O Father for Thy love which has loaned to us the presence of so sweet a treasure. May the memory console and uplift us as onward we move. Grant us Thy perfect radiance of Love and spiritual power. Amen.

Committal Service:

We commit this vacant body of clay to Mother Earth which gave it. Thus, casting petals of earthly flowers, do we consign it again to dust and ashes. With reverence and resigned remembrance, we gently lay it down to rest. Dear little spirit, now liberated from the vesture of earth, go forth with our love on thy heavenly mission into realms divine. And yet, often may thy love for us draw thee back to bless with spiritual presence those dear unto thee. May the songs of angels joyfully attend thee. Amen.

Benediction:

Now as we go from here, grant, O Father, thy sustaining arm to strengthen us that we stumble not. Renew our faith and trust in Thee; help us to listen to the choirs of angels which vibrate so close to our earth world. May their songs heal and bless us until that day when we shall again be united with the departed. Amen.

THE CROSSING

"And I sit and think when the sunset's gold
        Is flushing river, and hill, and shore,
I shall one day stand by the river cold,
        And list for the sound of the boatman's oar;
I shall watch for a gleam of the flapping sail;
        I shall hear the boat as it gains the strand;
I shall pass from sight with the boatman pale,
        To the better shore of the spirit land.
I shall know the loved who have gone before,
        And joyfully sweet will the meeting be,
When over the river, the peaceful river,
        The angel of death shall carry me."

—*Nancy Priest*

CROSSING THE BAR

Sunset and evening star,
And one clear call for me,
And may there be no moaning of the bar
When I put out to sea.

But such a tide as moving seems asleep,
Too full for sound and foam,
When that which drew from out the boundless deep,
Turns again home.

Twilight and evening bell,
And after that the dark,
And may there be no sadness of farewell,
When I embark.

For though from out our bourne of time and place
The flood may bear me far;
I hope to see my Pilot face to face
When I have crossed the bar.

—*Alfred Lord Tennyson*

SING, MY SOUL

Sing, sing, my soul, for upward flying
The living hues obscure the dying,
And brightly glowing overhead
The lights of Life o'er-veil the dead!
Sweet breath Elysian wafts the soul,
Eternal zephyrs float and roll,
For near at hand is Heaven's ground
And Heaven's joyous voices sound!
The welcome smiles of friends and kin
Are there to welcome and begin
Our advent in that land of bliss —
They greet us with affection's kiss.
Sing, sing, my soul, God's will is done,
His purpose wrought, His battle won:
For Death is conquered — is no more —
Life is the victory in store.

—Rev. Converse E. Nickerson

WHAT IF SOME MORNING?

What if some morning when the stars were paling,
And the dawn whitened and the East was clear,
Strange peace and rest fell on me from the presence
Of a benignant Spirit standing near;

And I should tell him as he stood beside me,
"This is our Earth—most friendly and most fair;
Daily its sea and shore through sun and shadow
Faithful it turns, robed in its azure air;

There is blest living here, loving and serving,
And quest of truth and serene friendship dear:
But stay not, Spirit! Earth has one destroyer—
His name is Death: flee lest he find thee here!"

And what if, then, while still the morning brightened,
And freshened in the elm the summer's breath,
Should gravely smile on me, the gentle angel,
And take my hand, and say, "My name is Death."

—Edward Roland Sill

THERE IS NO DEATH

There is no death! the stars go down
   To rise upon some other shore,
And bright in heaven's jewelled crown
   They shine forevermore.
There is no death! the dust we tread
   Shall change beneath the summer showers
To golden grain, or mellow fruit,
   Or rainbow-tinted flowers.
There is no death! the forest leaves
   Convert to life the viewless air;
The rocks disorganize to feed
   The hungry moss they bear.
And ever near us though unseen,
   The dear immortal spirits tread,
For all the boundless universe
   Is Life—"there are no dead." *Sir Edward Bulwer-Lytton*

AT LAST

When on my day of life the night is falling,
And, in the winds from unsunned spaces blown
I hear far voices, out of darkness calling
   My feet to paths unknown.
Thou who hast made my home of life so pleasant,
Leave not its tenant when its wall decay;
O Love Divine, O Helper ever-present,
   Be thou my strength and stay!
Be near me when all else is from me drifting;
Earth, sky, home's pictures, days of shade and shine,
And kindly faces to my own uplifting
   The love which answers mine.
I have but Thee, my Father! let Thy spirit
Be with me then to comfort and uphold,
No gate of pearl, no branch of palm I merit,
   Nor street of shining gold.
Suffice it if,—my good and ill unreckoned,
And both forgiven through Thy abounding grace—
I find myself by hands familiar beckoned
   Unto my fitting place.   *—John Greenleaf Whittier*

ONLY A THIN VEIL BETWEEN US

Only a thin veil between us,
My loved ones so precious and true,
Only a mist before sunrise,
I am hidden away from your view.
Often I come with my blessing
And strive all your sorrows to share,
At night when you're quietly sleeping
I kiss down your eyelids in prayer.

Chorus:

Only a thin veil between us,
Some morning the angels will come
And then in that bright land of beauty
We'll gather with loved ones at home,—
Home, beautiful home,
No longer in sadness to roam,
But safe in the kindom of glory,
We'll dwell with our loved ones at home.

Only a thin veil between us,
Not many longs years will it stay;
'Tis growing more fleecy and golden
As earth-life with you fades away;
And when you are thinking so sadly
Of days all so joyous and free,
It is then I am nearest, my darling,
And I bring sweetest comfort to thee.

Only a thin veil between us,
O cannot you see me just now,
I bring you a crown of rare flowers
With which to encircle your brow.
So long have I waited to greet thee
And tell of the joys that are mine,
Be true and be faithful to duty
And my home in its beauty is thine.

—*C. Payson Longley*

STILL, STILL WITH THEE

Still, still with Thee, when purple morning breaketh,
When the bird waketh, and the shadows flee;
Fairer than morning, lovelier than the daylight,
Dawns the sweet consciousness, I am with Thee.

When sinks the soul, subdued by toil, to slumber,
Its closing eyes look up to Thee in prayer;
Sweet the repose, beneath Thy wings o'er-shading,
But sweeter still, to wake and find Thee there.

So shall it be at last, in that bright morning,
When the soul waketh, and life's shadows flee;
O in that hour, fairer than daylight dawning,
Shall rise the glorious thought — I am with Thee.

Harriet Beecher Stowe

"Only the body dies and is laid in the dust. The spirit lives and will live forever in the shelter of God's love and mercy. But in this life, also, the loved ones continue in remembrance of those, to whom they were precious. Every act of goodness they performed, every true and beautiful word they spoke is treasured up and becomes an incentive to conduct by which the living honor the dead."

"There Is No Death"

"There is no death, there is no night,
The loved one, passed beyond our sight
Is living in eternal light
Removed from care and pain.
Some day, in a fairer land
We shall hear the voice,
We shall touch the hand,
And with lifted hearts, which understand,
We shall see our own again."

SELECTED QUOTATIONS:

Joseph Addison wrote:

"It must be so,—Plato, thou reasonest well!
Else whence this pleasing hope, this fond desire,
This longing after immortality?
Or whence this secret dread, and inward horror
Of falling into naught? Why shrinks the soul
Back on herself, and startles at destruction?
'T is the divinity that stirs within us;
'T is Heaven itself, that points out a hereafter,
And intimates eternity to man.
"Eternity!—thou pleasing, dreadful thought!
Through what variety of untried being,
Through what new scenes and changes, must we pass;
The wide, the unbounded prospect lies before me;
But shadows, clouds, and darkness rest upon it.
Here will I hold. If there's a Power above us
(And that there is, all Nature cries aloud
Through all her works), he must delight in virtue;
And that which he delights in must be happy.
But when? or where?
"But this informs me I shall never die.
The soul secured in her existence, smiles
At the drawn dagger, and defies its point.
The stars shall fade away, the sun himself
Grow dim with age, and Nature sink in years;
But thou shalt flourish in immortal youth,
Unhurt amid the war of elements,
The wreck of matter, and the crush of worlds!"

—from Cato's "Soliloquy."

Epictetus said, five centuries before Christ:

"If I am identical with my corpse, I shall be thrown out, (buried;) but if I am something more than the corpse, speak more handsomely, as the thing is, and do not think to frighten me. These things are frightful to children and fools. But if any one who has once entered into the school of a philosopher knows not what he himself is, then he deserves to be frightened, and to flatter the last object of flattery; if he has not yet learned that he is neither flesh, nor bones, nor nerves, but is that which makes use of these, and regulates and comprehends the phenomena of existence."

John Milton, great English poet and thinker, said:

"Millions of spiritual beings walk the earth both when we wake and when we sleep."

Cato (as quoted by Cicero), 243 B.C.:

"O glorious day, when I shall remove from this confused crowd to join the divine assemble of souls; for I shall go not only to meet great men, but also my son, his spirit looking back upon me, departed to that place, whither he knew that I should come; and he has never deserted me. If I have borne his loss with courage, it is because I consoled myself with the thought that our separation would not be for long."

Cicero, 106 B.C. said:

"When I consider the faculties with which the soul is endowed, its amazing celerity, its wonderful power of recollecting past events, its sagacity in discerning the future, together with its numberless discoveries in the arts and sciences, I feel a conscious conviction that this active apprehensive principle cannot possibly be of a mortal nature. I consider this world as a place nature never intended for a permanent abode, and I look on my departure from it as simply leaving an inn."

Homer's Iliad, 850 B.C.:

After the spirit of Patroclus had appeared and spoken to him in a dream, Achilles said:

" 'Tis true, 'tis certain man though dead, retains
Part of himself; the immortal mind remains:
The form subsists without the body's aid.
Aerial semblance, and an empty shade!
This night my friend, so late in battle lost,
Stood at my side, a pensive, plaintive ghost:
Even now familiar, as in life he came:
Alas, how different! yet how like the same!"

(Pope's translation: Book 23)

Victor Hugo, great French novelist, wrote:

"I feel in myself the future life. I am like a forest once cut
down; the new shoots are stronger and livelier than ever. I am
rising, I know, toward the sky. The sunshine is on my head. The
earth gives me its generous sap, but heaven lights me with the
reflection of unknown worlds. You say the soul is nothing but
the resultant of bodily powers. Why, then, is my soul more
luminous when my bodily powers begin to fail? Winter is on my
head, but eternal spring is in my heart. I breathe at this hour
the fragrance of the lilacs, the violets, and the roses, as at twenty
years. The nearer I approach the end, the plainer I hear around
me the immortal symphonies of the world that invites me. For
half a century I have been writing my thoughts in prose and in
verse; history, philosophy, drama, romance, tradition, satire, ode,
and song. But I feel I have not said the thousandth part of what
is in me. When I go down to the grave I can say 'I have finished
my work.' But I cannot say 'I have finished my life.' My day's
work will begin the next morning. The tomb is not a blind alley;
it is a thoroughfare. It closes on the twilight, it opens on the
dawn."

The Buddhist Scriptures declare:

"The Soul is myself; the body is only my dwelling place.
Death is not death; the soul merely departs and the body falls.
    The Soul is not born, it does not die; unborn eternal, it is
not slain, though the body be slain. Thinking of the Soul as
unbodily amongst bodies, and firm amongst fleeting things, the
wise man casts off his grief."

Plato, student of Socrates, born 426 B.C. wrote:

"The soul of each of us is an immortal spirit, and goes to other immortals to give an account of its actions. Can the soul be destroyed? No; but if in this present life it has shunned being governed by the body, and has governed itself, then it departs to that which resembles itself,—to the invisible, the divine, the wise, the immortal."

John the Revelator wrote:

"And I saw a new heaven and a new earth, for the first heaven and the first earth were passed away; and there was no more sea.

And God shall wipe away all tears from their eyes; and there shall be no more death, neither sorrow, nor crying, neither shall there be any more pain: for the former things are passed away."

Dr. Adam Clark, distinguished Methodist Commentator, in commenting upon Saul and Samuel (see his Commentaries, pp. 298-299) says:

"I believe Samuel did actually appear to Saul: and that he was sent to warn this infatuated king of his approaching death, that he might have an opportunity to make his peace with his Maker.

I believe there is a supernatural or spiritual world, in which human spirits, both good and bad, live in a state of consciousness.

I believe that any of these spirits may, according to the order of God, in the laws of their place of residence, have intercourse with this world and become visible to mortals."

Rev. Chauncey Giles, English Clergyman, declared:

"The spirit world is here, is everywhere around us, and is separated from us only by the thin veil of matter. We are in it now, though unconscious of it. Man is a spirit in the human form, and when the veil of matter is withdrawn, it reveals to him the spiritual world in which he was living before. He has not gone to any remote place. He is not changed. He sees the beings who were around him, and just as near him, before the veil was withdrawn from his eyes, as they are now. He does not go among strangers, and find everything new and wholly different from what he has seen and known before."

Seneca, the Roman Philosopher, born 58 B.C. said:

"When the day shall come that will separate this composition, human and divine, I will leave this body here, where I found it, and return to the gods. Not that I am altogether absent from them even now, though detained from superior happiness by this heavy earthly clog.

This short stay in mortal life is but the prelude to a better and more lasting life above. That which we call death is but a pause, or a suspension, and in truth a progress to life, only our thoughts look downward upon the body, and not forward upon the things to come.

That day which men are apt to dread as their last is but the birthday of an eternity."

Zoroaster said:

"The soul, being a bright fire, by the power of the Father, remains immortal; it will, in a manner, clasp God to itself."

Harrison D. Barrett; first president of the N.S.A. said:

Spiritualism gives us the phenomena, science and philosophy, which when blended in oneness, give to the world a religion that is provable both by induction and deduction, by scientific demonstration and spiritual revelation.

Pro. James H. Hyslop, American scientist, stated:

History shows that every intelligent man who has gone into an investigation of Spiritualism, if he gave it adequate examination at all, has come out believing in spirits; this circumstance places the burden of proof on the shoulders of the skeptic.

Sir Arthur Conan Doyle, author and keen observer of psychic manifestation, wrote:

"The religious aspect of Spiritualism is a system of thought and knowledge which can be reconciled with any religion. The basic facts are the continuity of personality, and the power of communication after death. These two basic facts are of as great importance to a Brahmin, a Mohammedan, or a Parsee, as to a Christian,—therefore Spiritualism makes a universal appeal."

The Rev. Lyman Abbot, editor and thinker, said:

I do not believe in a long dreary sleep, nor in a happy land, far, far away. I believe that death itself is a resurrection. Death is the dropping away of the body from the spirit or the resurrection of the spirit from the body; the two are identical. Death is as we see it here; resurrection is as they see it on the other side of the thin veil which separates the two worlds. I think I can truly say that I am never less lonely than when the choir invisible no longer seems invisible; when it seems to me as though I have only to open the door and enter into that other room where they are, unseen by me but not unable to see and minister to me.

Ignatius, native of Syria and a pupil of Polycarp, wrote:

Some in the church most certainly have a divine knowledge of things to come. Some have visions; others utter prophecies, and heal the sick by the laying on of hands; and others still speak in many tongues, bringing to light the secret mysteries, and innermost thoughts of men, and expounding the great things of God.

John Burroughs, American Naturalist, wrote:

"Under the influence of Sectarian Christianity, man has been taken out of the category of natural things, both in his origin and in his destiny. Saints have betrayed us, and Theologians have blackened and defaced our earthly temple.

Amid the decay of creeds, love of nature has high religious value. This has saved many persons in this world from mammon-worship, and from the frivolity and insincerity of the crowd. It has made them contented and at home everywhere in nature—in the house not made with hands. This home is their church, and the rocks and the hills are their altars, and the creed is written in the leaves of the trees and in the flowers of the fields and in the sands of the shore.

There are no heretics in Nature's church. The beauty of natural religion is that you have it at all times; you do not have to seek it in afar off myths and legends, in catacombs, in garbled texts, in miracles of dead saints, or wine-bibbing friars. It is of today and everywhere. The crickets chirp it, the birds sing it, the breezes chant it, the streams murmur it, the unaffected man lives it."

William Wadsworth wrote:

"Our birth is but a sleep and a forgetting;
The soul that rises with us, our life's star,
  Hath had elsewhere its setting
  And cometh from afar.
Not in entire forgetfulness,
And not in utter nakedness,
But trailing clouds of glory, do we come
From God who is our home."
"Thou, whose exterior semblance doth belie
  Thy soul's immensity!
Thou best philosopher, who yet doth keep
Thy heritage! thou eye among the blind,
That, deaf and silent, read'st the eternal deep,
Haunted forever by the Eternal Mind!"

Dr. James M. Peebles, lecturer and author, declared:

"Spiritualism, originating in God who is Spirit, and grounded in man's moral nature, is a substantial fact, and infinitely more— a fact plus reason and conscience; a fact relating to moral and religious culture—a sublime spiritual truth ultimating in consecration to the good, the beautiful, and the heavenly.

Spiritualism—a grand, moral science, and a wisdom religion —proffers the key that unlocks the mysteries of the ages. It constituted the foundation stones of all the ancient faiths. It was the vitalizing soul of all past religions. It was the mighty uplifting force that gave to the world in all ages its inspired teachers and immortal leaders.

Rightly translated, the direct words of Jesus are (John 4:24) —"Spirit is God." The spiritual is the real and the substantial. The spiritually minded are reverential."

Saint Paul wrote:

"We look not at the things which are seen, but at the things which are not seen; for the things which are seen are temporal; but the things which are not seen are eternal.

For we know that, if our earthly house of this tabernacle were dissolved, we have a building of God, a house not made with hands, eternal in the heavens."

Jesus Christ promised his disciples:

> "In my Father's house are many mansions, if it were not so, I would not have told you; I go to prepare a place for you that where I am there ye may be also. Let not your hearts be troubled, ye believe in God, believe also in me."

Washington Irving, distinguished American writer, said:

> "What could be more consoling than the idea that the souls of those we once loved were permitted to return and watch over our welfare? I see nothing in it (Spiritualism) that is incompatible with the tender and merciful nature of our religion, or revolting to the wishes and affections of the heart."

Professor Arthur H. Compton, scientist, declares:

> "The adventure and discipline of youth, the struggles and failures and successes, the pains and pleasures of maturity, the loneliness and tranquility of age, these make up the fire through which one must pass to bring out the pure gold of his soul. Having been thus perfected, what shall nature do with him? Annihilate him? What infinite waste! I prefer to believe one lives after death, continuing on a larger sphere, in co-operation with his Maker, the work he thus began here."

Dr. Pupin, noted scientist, emphasizes this statement:

> "The soul of a man is the highest product of God's creative handiwork. After God has spent untold time in creating man, and endowing him with a soul, which is the reflection of His image, is it reasonable to suppose that man lives here for a brief span and then is extinguished by death? That the soul has existed in vain?"

The Rev. William T. Manning, Episcopal Bishop, said:

> "The proof that our life in the future world is just as certain and real as the life we are now living, and we need to repent and prepare now for life in the other world. We will be the same persons we are now; death will not greatly change the character, soul and personality developed in this world. But in the other world we will stand in the light, nothing will be hidden, and we shall be seen as we are."

Rev. Harry Emerson Fosdick said in an Easter sermon:

"If the Easter hope is true, one has a great philosophy that makes a drama of life and there are forever and forever open doors ahead. But if it is not true, then a closed door is the ultimate symbol of the universe, a closed door for every individual life, a closed door for every generation's life, a closed door for all human life. We cannot avoid facing the two great philosophies: on the one side a universe of open doors, on the other a closed door as the final symbol of everything!"

Bishop R. S. Foster declares in a sermon:

"Earthly providence is a travesty of justice on any other theory than that it is a preliminary stage to be followed by rectifications. Either there must be a future, or consummate injustice sits upon the throne of the universe. This is the verdict of humanity in all ages."

Ovid, Roman Poet, 43 B.C., wrote:

"And now have I finished a work which neither the wrath of Jove, nor fire, nor steel, nor all-consuming time can destroy. Welcome the day which can destroy only my physical man in ending my uncertain life. In my better part I shall be raised to immortality above the lofty stars, and my name shall never die."

George Douglas, writer and thinker, said:

"Immortality! We bow before the very term. Immortality! Before it reason staggers, calculation reclines her tired head, and imagination folds her weary pinions. Immortality! It throws open the portals of the vast forever; it puts the crown of deathless destiny upon every human brow; it cries to every uncrowned king of men, 'Life forever is crowned for the empire of a deathless destiny!' "

Rev. Converse E. Nickerson, author and Spiritualist Evangelist, makes this statement:

"The ideal and objective of all religions must be God. Man must worship with his inner self,—the immortal part of him. The great spiritual 'words of God' fashion themselves in the moving emotions of the soul. The contemplation of God's power and His laws for man must extend their province just beyond the confines of the mortal and the material. God's Universe, being infinitely greater than man's realization or conception of it, causes the soul to thrill with the powerful imagination of what must lie ahead in the path of spiritual destiny. In the maze and glory of such grandeur the soul's never-ending existence sparkles with a dazzling splendor; immortality becomes a major fact in all philosophy and the eternal comfort of a perplexed humanity!"

Rev. Dr. Minot Simons:

"Our beliefs about the universe have changed, but the stars keep on shining. With all the changing forms of religious beliefs, the glory and significance of the things of spirit remain."

Rev. Phillips Brooks:

"The great majority of us amount to little and go through life unknown. For that great majority there is consolation only in our belief in immortality. There is no life so humble that if it be true and genuine, human and obedient to God, it may not hope to shed some of this light. There is no life so meagre that the greatest and wisest of us can afford to despise it. We can not know at what moment it may flash forth with the life of God."

Jacob Tarshish:

"The world is alive with unseen powers, which seemingly vanish, yet really come together again to be part of the stars and mountains, the rivers and oceans, bridges and skyscrapers. Trees die, blow bare to the cold of winter only to awaken to the sunshine of spring. Flowers die, yet something drops into the earth, is blanketed by the winter snow, and lifts its living head again, when rain and sun stir it into new color and beauty. The caterpillar wraps itself into a winding sheet, weaves the tangled web of his coffin cacoon, and is dead to the world. Then, lo! Spring comes to break the chrysalis and an altogether new creature, the butterfly wings thru the gentle breezes — a symbol of immortality. There is no death, only change. Death is a sleep and a forgetting, also a great adventure, a fulfilment of dreams, the gateway to another and more wonderful life."

Rev. Dr. John S. Bonnell:

"The individual, who organizes his life about the conception of eternal life, knows the joy of living for the Master's service and can face the bitterest blows of circumstance. In the promise of eternal life lies the greatest incentive for a full, rich, enduring life on earth."

Geo. D. Prentice:

"It cannot be that the earth is man's only abiding place. It cannot be that our life is a mere bubble cast up by eternity to float a moment on its waves and then sink into nothingness. There is a realm where the rainbow never fades and where the beautiful beings which now pass before us like shadows will stay in our presence forever."

Rev. Dr. Allen E. Claxton:

"Life after death is not a fond hope but an inevitable conclusion. Death is simply the doorway, by which we pass from one phase of this existence to another and it is no more mysterious than the manner in which we pass from infancy to youth and finally the adult graduates through death into everlasting life."

"The timeless essence of Christmas knows no season. It is not the creature of clock or calendar. It is not colored lights nor carols, the sound of bells, the tinseled tree. It is not a custom; neither is it a scarlet costume and white whiskers to be donned for a day, then laid back among the moth-balls. It does not come, tarry for a day and then disappear . . . It is Christmas wherever the human heart, touched by Him whose ever living spirit is the ever giving spirit, is moved to the expression of unselfish love."

The Easter season is typical of Life Eternal. It is the season of renewed hope and courage. Renewal of earth's fertility and the beauty of the flowers prove that there is no permanent Death.

THE NATURE OF THE SPIRIT WORLD

By Rev. Converse E. Nickerson

The spirit world is very real. It is as important in the circle of man's philosophy as is this planet earth, or any other planet in our solar system. It is as rational to consider the spirit world in a practical sense as it is to study and examine this natural world in which we dwell.

Upon our careful consideration of these facts rests in a very foundational way all hope and understanding of a future existence for the soul of man. Our philosophy of Spiritualism makes practical the consideration of Heaven and Angels. We do not confuse in some mythical manner our thoughts about the inhabitants of the spiritual spheres. If Angels have ever existed, they exist precisely at this moment; and they have a definite sphere of existence. Heaven, to us, is a reality that now is and ever has been. It does not dwell only in our imaginings about religion, or in some special chapter and text of the Bible. All the picturesque language describing Heaven is but the beautiful expressions of souls who have been there, or who long to taste of its grandeur and happiness. Heaven is a practically created realm, or it becomes no more important than a fairy tale.

Because we earnestly accept this truth regarding Heaven and Angels, we do affirm that our departed friends and loved ones also exist in spiritual spheres. We know that they must exist as personalities who once lived here with us; and that, too, we shall go to dwell with them and be exactly as they are.

Such an affirmation constitutes practical Spiritualism.

We are told by spirit visitors who entrance our mediums that there are many spheres of consciousness in the spirit world. Perhaps we may state the matter as "spheres" or conditions of consciousness. We know that here in our earth world we dwell in different conditions of consciousness; some of us are keenly conscious of spiritual things, while others make contact with the world about them through very limited material channels. The several "spheres" of consciousness here are brought about by the development of soul perception—or the lack of it. In proportion to our spiritual understanding we are quickened toward enlightenment of the soul within.

Then let us hold in our minds clearly the thought that "spheres" are created things: we can create a sphere for ourselves, dwell in it, and so come in touch with other harmonious states of like consciousness; in other words, we may mingle and co-mingle with those of the visible and invisible world according to the extent that we are attracted to them.

Since we do exist, we function in some degree of consciousness. It may be a distinct sphere and condition, or it may blend in graduated power and intensity with other spheres, above or below itself.

There is a great fundamental law of vibration. This law is an eternal one. It masters every created thing,—star, planet, and all connecting creations surrounding them.

All molecular activity is governed by the law of vibration. Atoms and whatever man shall discover about them—their power, quality, force and action—will all be under the law of vibration. It underlies all forces of motion—light, heat, cosmic ray, and every radiating form of energy that we yet know anything about.

Therefore, the soul of man, conditioned here in a garment of atoms, must be affected incessantly by vibratory forces.

The Thought World

Thought, the supreme transmitter of communication between individuals, is also subject to the law of vibration. We often use the term "impulse" as meaning an impelling force, or a sudden inclination; in reality it is the intelligent movement of Mind. All intelligent direction must be motivated by the soul through mind, and transmitted by the forces of vibration.

Soul being immortal and everlasting, it follows that thought and all the directive impulses of thought are continued beyond the physical senses as we know such senses here on the earth plane. The spirit world is peopled with thoughtful beings who engage in the pursuits of knowledge and the delights of companionship.

When we consider the wonderful truth that all the products of our science and invention have been originated by individual thought, we do not wonder that the spirit world will contain for us many blessings of a like quality with those we enjoy here. What we have here that has been of benefit to mankind—our houses, clothing, food, and scientific achievements—may find a counterpart in the spirit world.

The houses we live in here were first visualized in the mind of the person (or many persons) who first became inspired to invent them. Earth materials were here, but the secret of what they could become by invention and development, had to be relayed by the thoughts of man.

We expect a finer world in spirit. Its essences will be in a manner more delicate than those of earth; but withal they may be of a more lasting nature.

We think of electricity as being the most potent physical force known to us, and yet science knows of many material forces which are invisible to our physical senses that are more powerful than electricity.

Thoughts are things. Thoughts are powerful enough to utilize the hidden forces of nature, both here and in the spirit world. If thought has the power to transform the physical body from sickness to health, (and vice versa) it will also do like wonders for us when brought to bear upon forces and surroundings of the spirit world.

The apostle Paul advised: "Be ye transformed by the renewing of your mind."

Cicero, the noble thinker, said of the Soul: "It is the soul itself which sees and hears, and not those parts which are, as it were, but windows of the soul."

Our true perceptions must be perceived and analysed at the seat of life itself—the soul. It is there that we find consciousness, true personality, and the reality of being.

Spiritual Youth

There will be no such conditions as "old age" and decay in the spirit world. These forces are native only with the planet earth. Maturity, resourceful strength, spiritual vitality, and youthfulness will be the great blessings of that spirit existence!

It is the laws of physical growth here which bring about decay, for this is a form of old age and death; death is simply the name of that condition which describes the ceasing of organisms to function as such. When the working of the law of growth has spent itself, death is the result.

In the spirit world, where the change of death has been passed, there will be no possibility for the decay of organisms. Immortality means that state of being where death is passed away and the eternal life is begun.

The book of Revelation speaks of "the new heaven and the new earth." It also speaks of the passing away of all tears, all pain, and all sorrow. It declares that there will be no need for our solar sun to shine in the spirit realm, or for moon or stars by night—for there is no night there!

If these are the true descriptions of Heaven and the spirit world, then we must consider them as practical things and not as a visionary ideal of a religious creed.

The Color World

It is through the world of color that we gain our understanding of beauty. Infinite Mind has designed Light as the magic portal through which the soul sees beauty. We must remember that the eye, the organ of sight for the body, does not of itself discern beauty. It is only with the soul sight—or spiritual vision—that beauty is apprehended: the truth about the beauty of a rose does not consist in its color alone, but in the spiritual harmony it transmits to the soul-vision.

The rhythmical harmonies of color, intermingled with combinations of color blendings, give us great spiritual joy. Much of our pleasure here on earth is gained from the things that are beautiful; color and design delight us.

It is the same in comparison, when we consider music; its harmonious effect is on the soul, not the physical body; its melody is sensed and understood by the soul, not the physical body.

We will expect to find sweet melody and harmony; beauteous form and design and color, in the spirit world. The perfection of eternal youth will be reflected in these things of art and spiritual perfection.

The eternal principle of harmony in color and sound are echoed for us by Shakespeare, who causes Lorenzo in "The Merchant of Venice" to say:

> "How sweet the moonlight sleeps upon this bank!
> Here will we sit and let the sounds of music
> Creep in our ears: soft stillness and the night
> Become the touches of sweet harmony.
> Sit, Jessica. Look how the floor of heaven
> Is thick inlaid with patines of bright gold:
> There's not the smallest orb which thou beholdest
> But in his motion like an angel sings,
> Still quiring to the young-eyed cherubins;

Such harmony is in immortal souls;
But whilst this muddy vesture of decay
Doth grossly close us in, we cannot hear it."

Act v: Scene 1

The true realization of the spirit world must have a complete and solid foundation laid deep in the principles of reason and that eternal creative force which here we call science. The unlimited laws of eternal things will carry these principles infinitely further and far beyond our present powers of imagination.

The Infinite Mind of God cannot be revealed to us while we live in this limited sphere of earth and mortality. Only as we progress into realms of time and space, can we grow to understand or even glimpse the great wonders of the spirit world and our God-inherited future.

The Law of Righteousness

Jesus Christ came into this world to teach men how to heal their bodies of physical sickness and their souls of the imperfections of sin. The spiritual system that he taught them was called Righteousness. By the obtaining of a righteous life, man could raise himself to the spiritual mastery of almost every condition of this life. He could heal his physical body of deformity and weakness; he could become wise and conquering; he could experience the great Love of God the Father; he could become almost divine while walking in the garments of earth.

Inasmuch as man fails to develop his righteousness he is weak, impotent and spiritually blind. He does experience flashes of love, of wisdom, and of spiritual understanding; but they are only flashes of these great eternal truths. Man's human destiny is, for most of us on this earth plane, a struggle through the darkness and the night. But glimpses of spiritual truth are the true indications of the life to come; there is always the hope within that the sun-bright land of soul's desire lies just ahead.

The spirit world cannot be such a "sun-bright land" unless the full realization of spiritual power, love, and righteousness are found there.

We know that the blindness of sin keeps us from spiritual perfection; but we also know that through lack of wisdom and understanding we sin. If we knew better we would inevitably do better—at least we would make the effort towards a better way of life. It is our nature to desire the best, as it is also our nature to hope in the midst of adversity.

Since wisdom and understanding are not found here to the extent that righteousness is attained, we must expect that in the next expression of our lives we shall find the opportunities for spiritual perfection.

If we truly understood our friends and neighbors and kin, we would know how to love them as Jesus Christ has said we ought to love. Circumstances, jealousies, separating conditions of thoughts and ideals, make us strangers to one another. Many of these barriers will be unknown in the spirit world. Love was the center of the Christ doctrine. He taught love because he wanted us to fit ourselves for a future life in the spirit world. To that end he counseled: "Lay up treasures in heaven where neither moth nor rust doth corrupt, and where thieves do not break through and steal."—Matt. 6:19.

We must live through our lives here; that is inevitable. We must pass through the change called death and so on into another expression of life. That is also inevitable. Then the great message to all humanity should be "be prepared in this life for that greater and advanced expression of life in the spirit world."

We should look forward with quiet anticipation to some day arriving in that fairer world of beauty and spiritual happiness. Jesus Christ looked forward to the spirit world,—his Father's kingdom. He prayed for help to come to him from that place; he testified that its angels had given him strength and comfort when they came to minister unto him.

Spiritualism also testifies to that world and steadfastly considers it a place of spiritual health and mental understanding.

Our Christian brethren call it "The Land of Zion"; we call it The Spirit World.

WHAT IS PROPHECY?

By Rev. Converse E. Nickerson

Spiritualism's philosophy accepts the term "prophecy" exactly as the dictionary states it: namely, "a prediction of something to take place in the future, especially a prediction by Divine inspiration."

The Greek word from which our term comes is *prophemi*, meaning to foretell. *Pro* meaning before and *phemi*, to tell or to say. The Greeks therefore used the term prophet to mean "one who divines future events."

In the book of 1st Samuel, the 9th chapter, at the 9th verse, we read that prophecy is very definitely seership:

Beforetime in Israel, when a man went to enquire of God, thus he spake, Come, and let us go to the seer: for he that is now called a Prophet was before time called a Seer."

In the fifth chapter of 1st Thessalonians, verses 19 and 20 we find this command:

"Quench not the Spirit."
"Despise not prophesyings."

It is written in 1st Corinthians, chapters 14, verses 37 and 39, that Jesus the founder of the Christian gospel authorized the gift of prophecy:

"If any man think himself to be a prophet, or spiritual, let him acknowledge that the things that I write unto you are the commandments of the Lord, (Jesus). Wherefore, brethren, covet (desire) to prophesy, and forbid not to speak with tongues."

That Jesus was accustomed to use the gift of prophecy, is indicated in many incidents of his history. In Mark's account we read of the persecutors of Jesus "covering his face," and striking him, saying, "Prophesy unto us, thou Christ, Who is he that smote thee." (Combined verses of Mark, 15:65 and Matthew 26:28.)

In the 12th chapter of 1st Corinthians, Paul lists prophecy among the spiritual gifts:

"Now concerning spiritual gifts, brethren, I would not have you ignorant.
To another the working of miracles; to another prophecy; to another discerning of spirits; to another divers kinds of tongues; to another the interpretation of tongues." Verse 10.

An important instance of prophecy is related in the 14th Chapter of 1st Kings. Ahijah, the blind prophet, foretells events for the wife of Jeroboam, who comes to him in disguise at the behest of her husband, King Jeroboam.

To deny psychic manifestation is to deny the power of God.

Jesus Christ fulfilled such law by demonstrating the gift of prophecy which he possessed:

In the 17th chapter of Matthew there is recorded a most remarkable account of prophecy. The disciples were asked for tribute money; they in turn asked Jesus about it. Jesus said unto them:

> "Go thou to the sea and cast an hook and take up the fish that first cometh up; and when thou hast opened his mouth, thou shalt find a piece of money · that take and give unto them for me and thee." Matthew 17:27.

Another prophecy which Jesus made to his disciples is found in the beginning of the 21st chapter of Matthew:

> "And when they drew night unto Jerusalem and were come to Bethpage, unto the Mount of Olives, then sent Jesus two disciples,
> Saying unto them, Go into the village over against you, and straightway ye shall find an ass tied, and the colt with her. Loose them and bring them unto me.
> And if any man say ought unto you, ye shall say the Lord hath need of them; and straightway he will send them.
> And the disciples went and did as Jesus commanded them, and brought the ass and the colt and put on them their clothes, and they sat him thereon.
> And when he was come into Jerusalem, all the city was moved, saying who is this?
> And the multitude said, this is Jesus the prophet of Nazareth of Galilee."

In the gospel of Mark we read of the prophecy concerning the description of a man who was a stranger to the disciples and to Jesus, but who would, nevertheless, help them to find a certain house where they were to eat the Passover supper.

Mark, 14th chapter, verses 12th to 17th:
> "And the first day of unleavened bread, when they sacrificed the Passover, his disciples said unto him, Where wilt thou that we go

and prepare that thou mayest eat the Passover?
And he sendeth forth two disciples, and saith unto them, Go
ye into the city, and there shall meet you a man bearing a pitcher
of water: follow him. And wheresoever he shall go in, say ye to
the good man of the house, The Master saith, Where is the
guestchamber, where I shall eat the Passover with my disciples?
And he will show you a large upper room, furnished and prepared, there made ready for us.
And his disciples went forth, and came to the city, and found as
he had said unto them; and they made ready the Passover."

Spiritualism has only claimed the rightful powers that Jesus promised unto his disciples, for he said:

"Verily, verily, I say unto you, He that believeth on me, the
works that I do shall he do also; and greater works than these
shall he do."—John 14:12.

In our affirmation of Spiritualism as a RELIGION we thus dis-
tinguish it from the pagan world of spiritism. We believe that contact
with the spirit world is made by and through the avenues of mediumship,—psychic powers of clairvoyance, clairaudience and clairsentience.
Through these, and these alone, must come the information which,
when delivered to those on the mortal plane, constitutes the medium-
instrument as a prophet. The prophets, kings, and rulers of the Jews
were vested with this psychic rite because they foretold events and
communications concerning their nation and history, which were fulfilled. They professed to be in touch with the spirit world, although
sometimes the spirits they came into contact with were not of the
highest order, as the account given in the 22nd chapter of 1st Kings:

"A lying spirit in the mouth of all these thy prophets, etc."
Verse 23.

The soul passing through death does not by the process become
better either morally or intellectually, neither does it become worse in
its state of quality or consciousness. If the power and the conditions of
communication are met, then any spirit is permitted to return with a
communication.

It is the spiritual duty of the medium (prophet) that only the
most truthful and spiritually developed communicator from the spirit
world be allowed to communicate. If the privilege of communication
is abused then chaos and misunderstanding must follow. It is solely

through mediumship that the teachers and psychics can be the true leaders of the religion of Spiritualism.

Spiritualism is a spiritual religion and can be so interpreted when those who call themselves Spiritualists religiously demonstrate it.

We accept the advice of our spirit friends subject somewhat to the conditions of judgment which we ourselves are able to command. We understand that oftentimes our friends in spirit are able to warn, or to comfort, or to advise; but we must use our own sense of what is right and good for us, else we become merely the puppets of spirit direction with no will or judgment of our own.

The apostle Paul counsels, "try the spirit by the spirit."

RECORDED SPIRIT MANIFESTATIONS IN THE BIBLE

By Rev. Converse E. Nickerson

Throughout the Bible there are recorded definite evidences of communication between the planes of mortal existence and those of spirit. In nearly every chapter we find this evidence. Prophets and prophetesses swarm its pages as they chronicle the events which detail man's hope and his search for evidence of a future life.

Every phase of spirit communication is represented in many dramatic incidents in which figure most prominently the great names and leaders of Biblical antiquity. Psychic law, as we understand it today, undoubtedly prevailed in olden time, since God's laws have never changed. We have no intelligible key by which to read the meaning of the mysterious events occurring from Genesis to the end of Revelation, except that furnished by the truths of psychic phenomena. Angels, or spirit messengers, become the interpreters of Infinite Intelligence as it is revealed to man.

We are asked to believe in another life; there is no evidence of such a life without spirit communication to prove its existence. The details of that life are unfolded as we witness the appearances of spirit entities as they visit and comingle with man here on earth. These entities have but one source,—the spirit-world! To deny this truth is to refuse the vital evidence of the Bible. Upon that evidence man's complete faith in a future life for himself rests. Without that evidence the Bible becomes a meaningless record of obscure events.

The comfort of the New Testament is the affirmation of man's immortality. The surety of the Old Testament is the proof of it.

In Job we read: "There is a spirit in man: and the inspiration of the Almighty giveth them (him) understanding." (Job 32:8).

St. Paul tells us that "There is a natural body, and there is a spiritual body. Howbeit that was not first which is spiritual, but that which is natural, and afterward that which is spiritual." (1st Cor. 15: 44, 46).

Also we find the books of Psalms informing us that "He maketh His angels spirits." (Psalms 104:4).

St. Paul asks "Are they not all ministering angels?"

The book of Acts is the record of psychic events which began the work of the Christian church. In it we find many accounts of physical phenomena. The account of the haunted house where the disciples met to receive the first manifestation which was to be the sign that they were to begin their preaching and the works of their physical mediumship, is recorded in the 2nd chapter:

> "And suddenly there came a sound from heaven (the spirit-world) as of a rushing mighty wind, and it filled all the house where they were sitting.
> "And there appeared unto them cloven tongues like as of fire, and it sat upon each of them." (Verses 2 and 3).

The controlling spirits entranced them and "each spoke with a different language," as the Spirit gave them utterance. This is unmistakable as an instance of spirit manifestation!

The 12th chapter of Acts records the visitation of an angel to Peter while he is bound in prison. The angel releases him from his bonds and also opens the heavy gate of the city in order to completely liberate him;

> "When they were past the first and second ward, they came to the iron gate which leadeth into the city, which opened to them of its own accord, (spirit power) and they went out." (Acts 12:7, 10).

In the 10th chapter of Acts is the detailed record of Peter's trance and of the angel (spirit) who talked with him and directed him to go to Cornelius, an Italian. When Peter arrived at the house of Cornelius, he recounted his experience with the angel, and in turn Cornelius also told Peter of his spirit visitation.

> Cornelius said, "Four days ago I was fasting until this hour; and at the ninth hour I prayed in my house, and, behold, a man stood before me in bright clothing." (Acts 10:30).

In the 8th chapter we find Philip preaching to the eunuch and suddenly being caught away by spirit power:

> "And when they were come up out of the water, the Spirit of the Lord caught away Philip, that the eunuch saw him no more."
> (Acts, 8:39).

The central theme of this psychic book is the dramatic account of Paul's conversion; we read very vividly how Paul spoke with the risen spirit of Jesus on the road to Damascus. Because of this manifestation Paul began to believe definitely in the spirit-world and went forth to preach his great sermons on immortality and the future life. (22nd chapter of Acts.)

The remainder of the Book gives us the story of prophesies and angel appearances which carry Paul forward on his great mission. Anyone who reads and believes the Book of Acts must become converted to the truth of spirit communication; its statements are precise and complete and portray the psychic acts of the apostles.

PROPHECY AND MEDIUMSHIP

The first instance of Bible record where a medium is paid for his services, is found in the 9th chapter of 1st Samuel.

Saul, the son of Kish goes forth to seek the lost asses and is told of "a man of God" and how that "all that he saith cometh surely to pass." Saul and his servant decide to pay this "man of God for his services in finding the lost asses, so the servant informs Saul":

> "Behold, I have here at hand the fourth part of a shekel of silver; that will I give to the man of God, to tell us our way." (Verse 8)
> "Beforetime in Israel, when a man went to enquire of God, thus he spoke, Come let us go to the seer: for he that is now called a Prophet was beforetime called a Seer. (Verse 9)
> When Saul finds Samuel, the Seer declares:
> "I am the seer. . . .
> "As for time asses that were lost three days ago, set not thy mind on them; for they are found." (Verses 19, 20)

The great dramatic account of spirit manifestation which this book contains is found in the 28th chapter. After Samuel's physical death we read of Saul's seance with the Woman of Endor; her familiar spirit, or guide, pierces Saul's disguise and reveals to her that the king is before her. When the spirit of Samuel appears, the medium cries out:

> "I saw gods ascending out of the earth.
> "And he said unto her, what form is he of? And she said, an old man cometh up; and he is covered with a mantle. And Saul perceived that it was Samuel." (Verses 13, 14)

Samuel's spirit talks with Saul and delivered unto him a prophecy, telling him that on the morrow Saul and his three sons shall pass into spirit. This prophecy is fulfilled in chapter 31 when the sons are slain in battle and Saul, fearing disgrace to die by the enemy's hand, commits suicide by falling on his sword.

In the 14th chapter of 1st Kings we find mediumship and a prophecy:

> "At the time Abijah the son of Jeroboam fell sick.
> "And Jeroboam said to his wife, Arise, I pray thee and disguise thyself, that thou be not known to be the wife of Jeroboam; and get thee to Shiloh: behold there is Ahijah the prophet, which

told me I should be king over this people.

"... and go to him; he shall tell thee what shall become of the child.
"And Jeroboam's wife did so, and came to the house of Ahijah.
But Ahijah could not see; for his eyes were set by reason of his
age." (Verses 1, 2, 3 and 4)

Ahijah delivers to her a message of condemnation and sorrow,
telling her that the child shall die:

"Arise thou therefore, get thee to thine own house; and when
thy feet enter into the city, the child shall die." (Verse 12)
This prophecy was fulfilled to the letter. The child died.

ANGELS AND GUARDIAN SPIRITS

In the Book of Daniel we find many manifestations of angels;
throughout its twelve chapters Daniel, the Hebrew prophet, is visited
by angels from the higher spheres who show him the mysterious symbols and signs as they convey to him prophecies of future events.

In the early part of the book we find the account of the three cap-
tives being cast into the fiery furnace. When the king came to see if
they were consumed by the flames, he was astonished at seeing them
alive and not only them, but a fourth person, who, said the king's counsellors, was so bright and wonderful that he was "like the Son of God."
(Chapter 3, Verse 25)

In Chapter 5 we find the account of the hand writing on the wall
of Belshazzar's palace. The record reads:

"In the same hour came forth fingers of a man's hand, and wrote
over against the candlestick upon the plaster of the wall of the
king's palace; and the king saw the part of the hand that wrote."
(Verse 5)

Here is an instance of the materialized hand of a spirit. The record
does not say that it was God who wrote, but "the fingers of a man's
hand." This decidedly intimates that a spirit visitor was able to ma-
terialize part of himself. Evidently it was the spirit of a man who had
once lived upon the earth, — not one of the celestial angels of which
the book of Daniel so often speaks.

Daniel professed to worship "the God of Heaven." When his
political enemies (for he was favored above many in the kingdom),
prevailed against him, he was cast into a den of lions. Darius, then

the ruler had admired Daniel, and, with sorrow, went to the den to see if perchance Daniel had escaped the fury of the beasts. He found Daniel unharmed. In explanation, the Hebrew psychic said:

"My God hath sent his angel, and hath shut the lions' mouths, that they have not hurt me." (Chapter 6:22)

A guardian spirit had protected Daniel. At the circus the trainer of animals has control of the big beasts in the lions' cage; no other person is permitted to do his work. So it was, that a spirit who could control the lions was sent to guard Daniel.

HEALING

"They shall lay hands on the sick and they shall recover."
—Mark 16:18

"And Jesus put forth his hand and touched him, and immediately his leprosy was cleansed."—Matthew 8:3

And Peter said, "silver and gold have I none; but such as I have give I unto thee. In the name of Jesus Christ of Nazareth rise up and walk."

"And he took him by the right hand and lifted him up: and immediately his feet and ankle bones received strength.

"And he leaping up stood, and walked." Acts 3: 6, 7, 8)

In the Gospel of John we find an instance of spirit healing through the agency of a magnetized pool. The fifth chapter and 4th verse records it as follows:

"For an angel went down at a certain season into the pool, and troubled the water; whosoever then first after the troubling of the water stepped in was made whole of whatsoever disease he had."

Peter by miraculous healing power brought back the spirit of Tabitha, whom her friends believed dead:

"Peter put them all forth, and kneeled down, and prayed; and turning him to the body, said, Tabitha, arise. And she opened her eyes: and when she saw Peter, she sat up." Acts 9:40

WOMEN MEDIUMS

The Woman of Endor. 1st Samuel, 28
Miriam, the prophetess. Exodus 15:20
Huldah, the prophetess. 2nd Kings, 22nd:14th

Noadiah, the prophetess. Nehemiah, 6th :14th

Philip, the evangelist had four daughters who prophesied. Acts 21 :8 and 9.

Deborah, a prophetess who judged Israel. Judges, 4 :4

"A certain damsel possessed with a spirit of divination." Acts 16 :16

PROPHECIES

Moses and Elias foretell the trial and death of Jesus. Luke, 9 :30, 31

Jesus foretells the finding of a coin in a fishes' mouth. Matthew 17 :27

Jesus foretells the finding of the place for Passover feast of the Last Supper. Mark 14 :12, 13, 14

Jesus foretells the finding of the young colt with its mother, which he was to use in the triumphal entry into Jerusalem. Matthew 21 :1, 2, 3

Paul by spirit message foretells the shipwreck. Acts 27 :22

GIFTS OF THE SPIRIT

In 1st Corinthians Paul names the various gifts of mediumship, stating that "the manifestation of the Spirit is given to every man to profit withall" :

"For to one is given by the Spirit the word of wisdom ; to another the word of knowledge, by the same Spirit ;

"To another faith by the same Spirit ; to another the gifts of healing by the same Spirit ;

"To another the working of miracles ; to another prophecy ; to another discerning of spirits ; to another divers kinds of tongues ; to another the interpretation of tongues."

Rev. Moses Hull has recounted in detail much of the spiritual and physical phenomena of the Bible in his "Encyclopedia of Biblical Spiritualism." We refer the student to this most important volume.

No more valid authority among Christian people can Spiritualism have than the Bible. Since it is the one authoritative book that is the foundation of the Christian's faith in God, when it also becomes the Spiritualist's book of reference, it is supremely important.

The works of Jesus and his disciples compare exactly with those of gifted and inspired psychics and teachers of Spiritualism today.

QUESTIONS AND ANSWERS
CONCERNING SPIRITUALISM

What is a Spiritualist?

A Spiritualist is one who bases his religious beliefs on the truth of spirit communication. He believes that a correct understanding of the laws of Infinite Intelligence — God — are the foundation of true religion.

Are the Beliefs of Christianity Necessary for the Spiritualist?

One may be a believer in Spiritualism and omit the tenets of the Christian church. However, the knowledge which Spiritualism gives through the certainty that man survives the change called death should make complete Christian faith.

Is Spiritualism a Religion?

Spiritualism is a religion. It is also a Philosophy and a Science. It is a duly constituted religious body of worshippers, has many individual organizations in our own country, Canada, England, and other countries. Its churches and ministers have all the rights and privileges enjoyed by other religious denominations.

Is Spiritualism Recognized in the Scientific and Intellectual Circles of the World?

Yes. Many famous scientists have accepted the truth of physical phenomena. Prof. William Crookes, Sir Oliver Lodge, Alexis Carrel, Prof. Hyslop, and scores of others who stand high among their colleagues have openly made their affirmations in favor of Spiritualism. Poets and philosophers, ministers and other leaders in religious and intellectual fields have declared their views affirming their knowledge of individual soul communion.

How Should I Investigate Spiritualism?

By informing yourself of its facts through literature on the subject and by personal experience with mediums and teachers.

Where Can I Obtain Its Literature?

All public libraries have most of the world's great books which are written about Spiritualism and Psychic Phenomena. Apply to General Assembly of Spiritualists for lists of books and for periodicals dedicated to Spiritualism.

What Is the Meaning of the Term "Fortune-teller?"

A fortune-teller (forbidden by law) is one who automatically predicts events for personal gain and without regard to spiritual upliftment. Tea-cup readers, card readers, crystal gazers and elemental psychists are often in this class. The true psychic resorts to none of these agencies for describing psychic events, either past or present or in the future. Mediumship is a sacred and exalted gift of the spirit.

Can Fortune-tellers Possess Psychic Powers?

Yes. No true psychic needs the aid of any artificial means for the exercising of psychic power. The sensationalist often depends upon dramatic accessories in order to impress the public. There is no true prediction without psychic manifestation.

Is It Not the Purpose of Spiritualism to Predict the Future?

Spiritualism is of little use to humanity if its office is but to foretell future events. The test message which truly identifies a loved one in spirit should inspire reverence and thanksgiving, not the idle curiosity that accompanies a worker of magic.

Is Spirit Communication Necessary to Faith in a Future Life?

Yes. To be convinced of personal survival after death, something more than religious faith is necessary. Spiritualism proves that the soul of man survives death. Other religious faiths accept that fact only on faith. To "know for oneself and not for another," as Job puts it, clears away doubt and strengthens our desires toward spiritual perfection.

Why Do Many Mediums Possess Little Education?

The spiritual gift of mediumship does not depend upon education. The gift of eye-sight, or hearing, or sense of balance, as in color arrangement, are not dependent upon educational training. Psychic gifts of clairvoyance or clairaudience are natively born with the instrument and become developed through use, or some sudden mental release that makes the instrument conscious of such faculty.

Has Hypnotism Anything to do with Spiritualism?

Hypnotism has no connection whatsoever with the phenomena of Spiritualism.

Is Telepathy True?

Telepathy, or the transference of thought has been experimented with in some colleges of science. The tests made discovered nothing that our psychics had not been doing for years. There seems to be quite a difference between telepathy and so-called "mind-reading." Our minds are like radio stations and, when properly attuned can pick up impulses. Caution should be exercised against the improper use of the powers of telepathy.

Are Spirit Communications Always Correct?

Sometimes a message may be colored by the mind of the medium without the medium being conscious of it. When this occurs the intelligent medium will admit and explain. Most messages of identification are very direct and convince as to names,   ents and circumstances related.

Is Mediumship a Natural Gift?

Yes. Mediumship is subject to natural laws, as are all manifestations of nature whether in the material or the spiritual world. These laws must be undertsood and complied with.

How Do We Discover Psychic Ability?

Often psychic ability is discovered accidently by the person possessing it, or by some observer. Such ability depends upon use in order to strengthen and become dependable.

How is Official Recognition Secured?

The General Assembly of Spiritualists issues certificates of recognition to such as are eligible through study and tests of their mediumship. Our psychics correspond to the clergy of other denominational churches. We have Ordained Ministers, Licentiates, Associate Ministers, and Healers.

Do All Souls Have Opportunity for Progression?

Yes. We teach that "The Doorway To Reformation Is Never Closed Against Any Human Soul Here Or Hereafter." Every human soul that is born into life is a child of God. There is neither refusal nor hindrance for progression on the great soul pilgrimage toward the heights of perfection.

What Set of Principles Does Spiritualism Proclaim?

The General Assembly of Spiritualists has adopted what is known as its "Declaration of Principles." These principles consist of eight and may be found in this Manual.

How Does the Philosophy of Spiritualism Define the Miracles of The Bible?

It teaches that all manifestation must come under natural laws. Many of the so-called miracles of the Bible are supported only by tradition. The "healing" and casting out of "devils" we believe were manifestations of psychic power.

Can Ill-Disposed Spirits Harm Us?

Only in the same way that evil companions can bring harm. Your associates have a direct influence for good or evil. Like attracts like, and so it is with spirit forces: if we spiritually ask for only the highest, the evil can find no companionship with us. Prayer and pure desires are safe-guards

Is There a Heaven, a Purgatory or a Hell in the Spirit World?

Our philosophy does not teach of Purgatory. We believe in conditions of darkess and unrest in the spirit world. These may be termed conditions of Hell. We believe that every soul is rewarded or punished by the great law of Compensation; but not punished as a form of vengeance by an angry God. Heaven is a state of spiritual contentment and happiness; the Spirit World is the universal state of spiritual (or spirit) existence. Into this state all emancipated souls enter upon leaving the physical body. We believe that the world of spirit permeates the entire universe. It is as real and tangible to those who have passed into it as are this life and world to us.

If There is No Hell How are the Evil Punished?

All states of evil are states of ignorance. Our acts, either good or bad, produce direct results. Thus acts which bring about injury to others react upon the doer; sometimes physically, but always spiritually. Such evil acts limit and retard the spiritual progress of the doer. The Scriptural sage declared: "Keep thy heart with all diligence, for out of it are all the issues of life."

Does the Religion of the Spiritualist Accept "Vicarious Atonement?"

Spiritualism teaches personal responsibility. Every one must work out his own salvation, striving toward spiritual perfection. Equal opportunity is given for this by the free will which may choose good from evil. God does not require a blood sacrifice to appease Him, for God is eternally merciful, eternally loving, and eternally the true spiritual Father of His created children.

Will Not Such Teachings Encourage Selfishness and Crime?

They will produce exactly the opposite. When we know that "death" does not release us from personal responsibility, both toward ourselves and God, we will then feel more disposed to avoid doing evil and seek that which is good. Knowledge and effort will become part of our desires toward spiritual perfection.

Should the Bible be Taught in Spiritualist Churches?

The beautiful and spiritually valuable things of the Bible should be emphasized in the Religion of the Spiritualist. The New Testament especially is a valuable handbook of the Spiritualist Religion. Unless we recognize this central source of spiritual instruction we will fail to deserve the respect and friendship of Orthodox Christianity. It is important that we hold to the finest standards of spiritual truth.

What do Spiritualists Believe about Other Sacred Books of Eastern Religions?

We believe these have their place with the peoples who are by nature of their several races best fitted to benefit by them. Until we have mastered the spiritual books of instruction which are at hand, we lose time and opportunity to study the cults and religions of the East.

How Can We Become Better Spiritualists?

By sincerely accepting Spiritualism as our religion. By making a study of its principles of truth and applying them to our daily lives. To be intelligent Spiritualists we must read and understand what we read. To be spiritual Spiritualists we must religously worship God through our understanding of the Philosophy of Spiritualism. To be progressive Spiritualists we must work for Spiritualism — become members of its churches; regularly attend and support the particular church we hold membership in; abjure all fraud and deception and promptly denounce it. Love God and keep His Commandments, and seek for all good.

SELECTED POETRY

IF YOU WOULD LOOK FOR ME

If you would look for me
    When I am gone,
Look not among the dead, but happily
Follow the trail of my memory;
    Look to what I've done.

My spirit swift as light will go
    — If you are seeking —
Back to the scenes of long ago;
The joys and sorrows I used to know,
    Always I'll be seeking.

Be sure I'll seek the places
    That I have ever known;
You'll see me 'mongst friendly faces;
About my books and papers, I'll leave traces,
    When I am gone.
                —Mable Hall Shaner

IF WE KNEW EACH OTHER

If I knew you and you knew me —
If both of us could clearly see,
And with an inner light divine
The meaning of your heart and mine —
I'm sure that we would differ less,
And clasp our hands in friendliness;
Our thoughts would pleasantly agree,
If I knew you and you knew me.

REVEALMENT

A breath of the glory of summer
    Sweeps over my soul today,
Though the winds are searching and tireless
    And the winter skies are gray.
But beyond all the gloom and the shadows
    The fragrance and beauty arise,
And I tread, by some magic and music,
    In the pathways of Paradise.

Lillian Whiting

I AM NOT DEAD

I go to life, not death, —
From darkness to life's native sky;
I go from sickness and from pain
To health and immortality.

I wait amid a shining clime
Where God's pure light is shed,
I wait and beckon you to come, —
I live, I am not dead!

Sometimes I touch your hands and smile,
I greet you deathlessly;
My love continues to extend
Across the spaces endlessly.

I will see your tears, I will feel your prayers, —
But look beyond the pale of clay;
I am not dead. On through the years
We shall continue in God's day!

—Converse E. Nickerson

A W A Y

I cannot say, and I will not say
That he is dead. He is just away!

With a cheery smile, and a wave of the hand
He has wandered into an unknown land,

And left us dreaming how very fair
It needs must be, since he lingers there.

And you — O you, who the wildest yearn
For the old-time step and the glad return, —

Think of him faring on, as dear
In the love of There as the love of Here;

Mild and gentle, as he was brave, —
When the sweetest love of his life he gave

To simple things:—Where the violets grew
Blue as the eyes they were likened to,

The touches of his hands have strayed
As reverently as his lips have prayed:

When the little brown thrush that harshly chirred
Was dear to him as the mocking-bird;

And he pitied as much as a man in pain
A writhing honey-bee wet with rain,

Think of him still the same, I say:
He is not dead — he is just away!

—James Whitcomb Riley

WHY SHOULD WE WEEP FOR THOSE WHO DIE?

Why should we weep for those who die?
    They fall, their dust returns to dust;
Their souls shall live eternally
    Within the mansions of the just.
They die to live, they sink to rise,
    They leave this wretched mortal shore;
But brighter suns and brighter skies
    Shall smile on them for evermore.

Why should we sorrow for the dead?
    Our life on earth is but a span;
They tread the path that all must tread,
    They die the common death of man.
The noblest songster of the dale
    Must cease when winter's frowns appear;
The reddest rose is wan and pale
    When autumn tints the changing year.

The fairest flowers on earth must fade,
    The richest hopes on earth must die;
Why should we mourn that man was made
    To droop on earth, but dwell on high?
The soul, the eternal soul, must reign
    In worlds devoid of pain and strife;
Then why should mortal man complain
    Of death, which leads to happier life?

—Alfred Lord Tennyson

SHOULD YOU GO FIRST

Should you go first and I remain
    To walk the road alone,
I'll live in memory's garden, dear,
    With happy days we've known.
In spring I'll wait for roses red
    When fades the lilac blue,
In early fall when brown leaves call
    I'll catch a glimpse of you.

Should you go first and I remain
    For battles to be fought,
Each thing you've touched along the way
    Will be a hallowed spot.
I'll hear your voice, I'll see you smile,
    Though blindly I may grope,
The memory of your helping hand
    Will buoy me up with hope.

Should you go first and I remain
    To finish with the scroll,
No length'ning shadows shall creep in
    To make this life seem droll.
We've known so much of happiness,
    We've had our cup of joy,
And memory is one gift of God
    That death cannot destroy.

Should you go first and I remain,
    One thing I'd have you do,
Walk slowly down the path of death,
    For soon I'll follow you.
I'll want to know each step you take
    That I may walk the same,
For some day down that lonely road
    You'll hear me call your name.

—Albert Kennedy Rowswell

"THE TWILIGHT BELL OF THE ANGELS"

There has come to my mind a legend, a thing I half
    forgot,
And whether I read it or dreamed it, — ah, well, it
    matters not.

It's said that in heaven at twilight a great bell softly
    swings,
And man may listen and harken to the wonderful music
    that rings,
If he puts from his heart's inner chamber all the passion
    and pain and strife,
Heartaches and weary longing, that throb in the pulses
    of life;
If he thrusts from his soul all hatred, all thoughts of
    wicked things,
He can hear in the holy twilight how the bell of the angel
    rings.

And I think there is in this legend, if we open our eyes
    to see,
Somewhat of an inner meaning, my friend, for you and
    me;
Let's look in our hearts and question, "Can pure thoughts
    enter in
To a soul if it be already the dwelling of thoughts of
    sin?"
So, then, let us ponder a little; let us look in our hearts
    and see
If the twilight bell of the angels could ring for you and
    me.

—Anon

THOUGHTS OF A FUTURE STATE

How shall I know thee in the sphere which keeps
The disembodied spirits of the dead,
When all of thee that time could wither sleeps ·
And perishes among the dust we tread?

Yet though thou wearest the glory of the sky,
Wilt thou not keep the same beloved name,
The same fair, thoughtful brow and gentle eye,
Lovelier in heaven's sweet climate, yet the same?

Shalt thou not teach me in that calmer home
The vision that I learned so ill in this —
The wisdom which is love — till I become
Thy fit companion in that land of bliss?

—*William Cullen Bryant*

HAUNTED HOUSES

All houses wherein men have lived and died
    Are haunted houses. Through the open door
The harmless phantoms glide.
    With feet that make no sound upon the floor.

There are more guests at table than the host
    Invited; the illuminated hall
Is thronged with quiet inoffensive ghosts
    As silent as the pictures on the wall.

The spirit-world around this world of sense
    Floats like an atmosphere, and everywhere
Wafts through these mists and vapors dense
    A vital breath of more ethereal air.

—*Henry W. Longfellow*

FROM "SNOW-BOUND"

Yet love will dream, and Faith will trust,
(Since He who knows our need is just.)
That somehow, somewhere, meet we must.
Alas for him who never sees
The stars shine through his cypress-trees!
Who, hopeless, lays his dead away,
Nor looks to see the breaking day
Across the mournful marbles play!
Who hath not learned, in hours of faith,
The truth to flesh and sense unknown,
That Life is ever lord of Death,
And Love can never lose its own!

—John Greenleaf Whittier

THE VOYAGEUR

There is a plan far greater than the one you know,
There is a landscape broader than the one you see,
There is a haven where the storm-tossed souls may go,
You call it death — we — Immortality.

You call it death, this seeming endless sleep,
We call it birth, the soul at last is free,
'Tis hampered not by time or space. You weep,
Why weep at death — 'tis Immortality.

Farewell, dear Voyageur — 'twill not be long,
Your work is done — now may peace rest with thee.
Your kindly thoughts and deeds, they will live on.
This is not death — 'tis Immortality.

Farewell, dear Voyageur — the river winds and turns,
The cadence of your song wafts near to me,
And now you know the thing that all men learn;
There is no death; there's Immortality.

—From "Walter" in "Voices From Beyond"

NO SOUL IS LOST

If barren trees can bud again
And blossoms pierce earth's frozen crust,
Why should a human soul in death
Go out, dissolve as crumbling dust?

Yet there are those who still affirm
That some must perish, writhe in pain,
While others know eternal bliss,
Absolved from every earthly stain.

Oh, that all men could understand!
No "wrath of God" metes punishment
But only ignorance of Truth;
By erring thoughts our woes are sent.

There is for all a glad rebirth —
Nature herself this promise gives —
For heaven's within each human breast:
No soul is lost but ever lives!

—Lucile Chandler

THE ARROW AND THE SONG

I shot an arrow into the air,
It fell to earth, I knew not where;
For, so swiftly it flew, the sight
Could not follow it in its flight.

I breathed a song into the air,
It fell to earth, I knew not where;
For who has sight so keen and strong,
That it can follow the flight of a song?

Long, long afterward, in an oak
I found the arrow, still unbroke;
And the song, from beginning to end,
I found again in the heart of a friend.

—Henry W. Longfellow

THE BEYOND

It seemeth such a little way to me
Across to that strange country — The Beyond;
And yet, not strange, for it has grown to be
The home of those of whom I am so fond;
They make it seem familiar and most dear,
As journeying friends bring distant regions near.

So close it lies, that when my sight is clear
I think I almost see the gleaming strand.
I know I feel those who have gone from here
Come near enough sometimes, to touch my hand.
I often think, but for our veiled eyes,
We should find Heaven right 'round about us lies.

I never stand above a bier and see
The seal of death set on some well-loved face,
But that I think, "One more to welcome me
When I shall cross the intervening space;
Between this land and that one over there;
One more to make the strange Beyond seem fair."

And so for me there is no sting of death,
And so the grave has lost its victory.
It is but crossing, with a bated breath,
And white, set face, a little strip of sea,
To find the loved ones waiting on the shore,
More beautiful, more precious than before.

—*Ella Wheeler Wilcox*

DIVINE PROMISE

I have learned
This doctrine from the vanishing of youth,
The pictured primer, true, is thrown aside;
But its first lesson liveth in my heart:
I shall go on through all eternity.
Thank God, I am only an embryo still;
The small beginning of a glorious soul,
An atom that shall fill immensity!

—A C. Coxe

SHE LIVES

Her sufferings ended with the day;
    Yet lived she at its close,
And breathed the long, long night away
    In statue-like repose.

But when the sun, in all its state,
    Illumined the eastern skies,
She passed through glory's morning-gate,
    And walked in Paradise!

—James Aldrich

Of Heaven and Earth: Essays Presented at the First Sitchin Studies Day, edited by Zecharia Sitchin. ISBN 1-885395-17-5 • 164 pages • 5 1/2 x 8 1/2 • trade paper • illustrated • $14.95

God Games: What Do You Do Forever?, by Neil Freer. ISBN 1-885395-39-6 • 312 pages • 6 x 9 • trade paper • $19.95

Space Travelers and the Genesis of the Human Form: Evidence of Intelligent Contact in the Solar System, by Joan d'Arc. ISBN 1-58509-127-8 • 208 pages • 6 x 9 • trade paper • illustrated • $18.95

Humanity's Extraterrestrial Origins: ET Influences on Humankind's Biological and Cultural Evolution, by Dr. Arthur David Horn with Lynette Mallory-Horn. ISBN 3-931652-31-9 • 373 pages • 6 x 9 • trade paper • $17.00

Past Shock: The Origin of Religion and Its Impact on the Human Soul, by Jack Barranger. ISBN 1-885395-08-6 • 126 pages • 6 x 9 • trade paper • illustrated • $12.95

Flying Serpents and Dragons: The Story of Mankind's Reptilian Past, by R.A. Boulay. ISBN 1-885395-38-8 • 276 pages • 6 x 9 • trade paper • illustrated • $19.95

Triumph of the Human Spirit: The Greatest Achievements of the Human Soul and How Its Power Can Change Your Life, by Paul Tice. ISBN 1-885395-57-4 • 295 pages • 6 x 9 • trade paper • illustrated • $19.95

Mysteries Explored: The Search for Human Origins, UFOs, and Religious Beginnings, by Jack Barranger and Paul Tice. ISBN 1-58509-101-4 • 104 pages • 6 x 9 • trade paper • $12.95

Mushrooms and Mankind: The Impact of Mushrooms on Human Consciousness and Religion, by James Arthur. ISBN 1-58509-151-0 • 103 pages • 6 x 9 • trade paper • $12.95

Vril or Vital Magnetism, with an Introduction by Paul Tice. ISBN 1-58509-030-1 • 124 pages • 5 1/2 x 8 1/2 • trade paper • $12.95

The Odic Force: Letters on Od and Magnetism, by Karl von Reichenbach. ISBN 1-58509-001-8 • 192 pages • 6 x 9 • trade paper • $15.95

The New Revelation: The Coming of a New Spiritual Paradigm, by Arthur Conan Doyle. ISBN 1-58509-220-7 • 124 pages • 6 x 9 • trade paper • $12.95

The Astral World: Its Scenes, Dwellers, and Phenomena, by Swami Panchadasi. ISBN 1-58509-071-9 • 104 pages • 6 x 9 • trade paper • $11.95

Reason and Belief: The Impact of Scientific Discovery on Religious and Spiritual Faith, by Sir Oliver Lodge. ISBN 1-58509-226-6 • 180 pages • 6 x 9 • trade paper • $17.95

William Blake: A Biography, by Basil De Selincourt. ISBN 1-58509-225-8 • 384 pages • 6 x 9 • trade paper • $28.95

The Divine Pymander: And Other Writings of Hermes Trismegistus, translated by John D. Chambers. ISBN 1-58509-046-8 • 196 pages • 6 x 9 • trade paper • $16.95

Theosophy and The Secret Doctrine, by Harriet L. Henderson. Includes *H.P. Blavatsky: An Outline of Her Life,* by Herbert Whyte, ISBN 1-58509-075-1 • 132 pages • 6 x 9 • trade paper • $13.95

The Light of Egypt, Volume One: The Science of the Soul and the Stars, by Thomas H. Burgoyne. ISBN 1-58509-051-4 • 320 pages • 6 x 9 • trade paper • illustrated • $24.95

The Light of Egypt, Volume Two: The Science of the Soul and the Stars, by Thomas H. Burgoyne. ISBN 1-58509-052-2 • 224 pages • 6 x 9 • trade paper • illustrated • $17.95

The Jumping Frog and 18 Other Stories: 19 Unforgettable Mark Twain Stories, by Mark Twain. ISBN 1-58509-200-2 • 128 pages • 6 x 9 • trade paper • $12.95

The Devil's Dictionary: A Guidebook for Cynics, by Ambrose Bierce. ISBN 1-58509-016-5 • 144 pages • 6 x 9 • trade paper • $12.95

The Smoky God: Or The Voyage to the Inner World, by Willis George Emerson. ISBN 1-58509-067-0 • 184 pages • 6 x 9 • trade paper • illustrated • $15.95

A Short History of the World, by H.G. Wells. ISBN 1-58509-211-8 • 320 pages • 6 x 9 • trade paper • $24.95

The Voyages and Discoveries of the Companions of Columbus, by Washington Irving. ISBN 1-58509-500-1 • 352 pages • 6 x 9 • hard cover • $39.95

History of Baalbek, by Michel Alouf. ISBN 1-58509-063-8 • 196 pages • 5 x 8 • trade paper • illustrated • $15.95

Ancient Egyptian Masonry: The Building Craft, by Sommers Clarke and R. Engelback. ISBN 1-58509-059-X • 350 pages • 6 x 9 • trade paper • illustrated • $26.95

That Old Time Religion: The Story of Religious Foundations, by Jordan Maxwell and Paul Tice. ISBN 1-58509-100-6 • 103 pages • 6 x 9 • trade paper • $12.95

The Book of Enoch: A Work of Visionary Revelation and Prophecy, Revealing Divine Secrets and Fantastic Information about Creation, Salvation, Heaven and Hell, translated by R. H. Charles. ISBN 1-58509-019-0 • 152 pages • 5 1/2 x 8 1/2 • trade paper • $13.95

The Book of Enoch: Translated from the Editor's Ethiopic Text and Edited with an Enlarged Introduction, Notes and Indexes, Together with a Reprint of the Greek Fragments, edited by R. H. Charles. ISBN 1-58509-080-8 • 448 pages • 6 x 9 • trade paper • $34.95

The Book of the Secrets of Enoch, translated from the Slavonic by W. R. Morfill. Edited, with Introduction and Notes by R. H. Charles. ISBN 1-58509-020-4 • 148 pages • 5 1/2 x 8 1/2 • trade paper • $13.95

Enuma Elish: The Seven Tablets of Creation, Volume One, by L. W. King. ISBN 1-58509-041-7 • 236 pages • 6 x 9 • trade paper • illustrated • $18.95

Enuma Elish: The Seven Tablets of Creation, Volume Two, by L. W. King. ISBN 1-58509-042-5 • 260 pages • 6 x 9 • trade paper • illustrated • $19.95

Enuma Elish, Volumes One and Two: The Seven Tablets of Creation, by L. W. King. Two volumes from above bound as one. ISBN 1-58509-043-3 • 496 pages • 6 x 9 • trade paper • illustrated • $38.90

The Archko Volume: Documents that Claim Proof to the Life, Death, and Resurrection of Christ, by Drs. McIntosh and Twyman. ISBN 1-58509-082-4 • 248 pages • 6 x 9 • trade paper • $20.95

The Lost Language of Symbolism: An Inquiry into the Origin of Certain Letters, Words, Names, Fairy-Tales, Folklore, and Mythologies, by Harold Bayley. ISBN 1-58509-070-0 • 384 pages • 6 x 9 • trade paper • $27.95

The Book of Jasher: A Suppressed Book that was Removed from the Bible, Referred to in Joshua and Second Samuel, translated by Albinus Alcuin (800 AD). ISBN 1-58509-081-6 • 304 pages • 6 x 9 • trade paper • $24.95

The Bible's Most Embarrassing Moments, with an Introduction by Paul Tice. ISBN 1-58509-025-5 • 172 pages • 5 x 8 • trade paper • $14.95

History of the Cross: The Pagan Origin and Idolatrous Adoption and Worship of the Image, by Henry Dana Ward. ISBN 1-58509-056-5 • 104 pages • 6 x 9 • trade paper • illustrated • $11.95

Was Jesus Influenced by Buddhism? A Comparative Study of the Lives and Thoughts of Gautama and Jesus, by Dwight Goddard. ISBN 1-58509-027-1 • 252 pages • 6 x 9 • trade paper • $19.95

History of the Christian Religion to the Year Two Hundred, by Charles B. Waite. ISBN 1-885395-15-9 • 556 pages • 6 x 9 • hard cover • $25.00

Symbols, Sex, and the Stars, by Ernest Busenbark. ISBN 1-885395-19-1 • 396 pages • 5 1/2 x 8 1/2 • trade paper • $22.95

History of the First Council of Nice: A World's Christian Convention, A.D. 325, by Dean Dudley. ISBN 1-58509-023-9 • 132 pages • 5 1/2 x 8 1/2 • trade paper • $14.95

The World's Sixteen Crucified Saviors, by Kersey Graves. ISBN 1-58509-018-2 • 436 pages • 5 1/2 x 8 1/2 • trade paper • $29.95

ALSO AVAILABLE FROM THE BOOK TREE

Lightning Source UK Ltd.
Milton Keynes UK
UKOW02f1152241016

285994UK00001B/55/P